CAKE POPS

Birthdays · Engagements · Weddings · Holidays

Published in 2013 by ACP Books, Sydney
ACP Books are published by ACP Magazines Limited,
a division of Nine Entertainment Co.

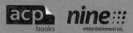

ACP BOOKS

Publishing director, ACP Magazines Gerry Reynolds
Publisher Sally Wright
Editorial & food director Pamela Clark
Creative director Hieu Chi Nguyen
Art director & designer Hannah Blackmore
Food concept director Sophia Young
Editor Abby Pfahl
Food editor Alexandra Elliott
Contributing writer Rosie Fittler
Sales & rights director Brian Cearnes
Marketing manager Bridget Cody
Senior business analyst Rebecca Varela
Operations manager David Scotto
Production controller Corinne Whitsun-Jones

Published by ACP Books, a division of
ACP Magazines Ltd, 54 Park St, Sydney;
GPO Box 4088, Sydney, NSW 2001.
phone (02) 9282 8618; fax (02) 9126 3702
acpbooks@acpmagazines.com.au;
www.acpbooks.com.au

Photographer Maree Homer
Stylist Louise Bickle
Photochef Adam Cremona
Recipe development Lucy Nunes, Elizabeth Macri,
Emma Braz, Adam Cremona
Junior home economist Charlotte Binns-McDonald

The publisher would like to thank *Emerald + Ella* for
props used in photography (emeraldandella.com.au);
and *Glasshouse Cakes & Supplies* for specialty cake
decorations (glasshousecakes.com.au).

Printed by C&C Offset Printing, China.

Australia Distributed by Network Services,
phone +61 2 9282 8777; fax +61 2 9264 3278;
networkweb@networkservicescompany.com.au
New Zealand Distributed by Southern Publishers
Group, phone +64 9 419 2635; fax +64 9 419 2634
hub@spg.co.nz
South Africa Distributed by PSD Promotions,
phone +27 11 392 6065/6/7; fax +27 11 392 6079/80;
orders@psdprom.co.za

Title: Cake Pops / Food director, Pamela Clark.
ISBN: 978-1-74245-382-8 (pbk).
Notes: Includes index.
Subjects: Cake, cake decorating, icings.
Other authors/contributors: Clark, Pamela.
Also titled: The Australian Women's Weekly.
Dewey number: 641.8653

© ACP Magazines Ltd 2013
ABN 18 053 273 546

To order books
phone 136 116 (within Australia) or
order online at www.acpbooks.com.au
send recipe enquiries to
recipeenquiries@acpmagazines.com.au

THE AUSTRALIAN
Women's Weekly

CAKE POPS

Birthdays • Engagements • Weddings • Holidays

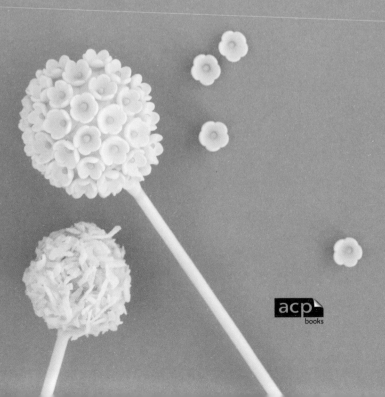

acp
books

CONTENTS

Before you begin

Cake pops are fiddly to make, but well worth the effort. Allow yourself plenty of time and call on family or friends to help you decorate and make it a fun occasion. Choose a simple cake pop to start with and once you've mastered that you'll be ready to tackle slightly trickier versions.

GETTING STARTED

• Most of these cake pops are decorated with supermarket staples, however a trip to a good cake decorating supplier will inspire you and can make decorating easier. If you don't have a store near you, try ordering decorations online.

• Once balls of cake are coated with icing or melted chocolate, they need to dry without touching any surface. Stand the pops upright in a thick styrofoam block, available from cake decorating suppliers.

If you can't find styrofoam, use some old egg cartons. Make holes in the top with a skewer or small knife, just large enough to hold the sticks upright. You will need to make sure you have this in place before you start dipping the cake pops.

• Cake pop sticks (also sold as "lollipop candy sticks") are available from cake decorating suppliers and craft shops. You can also use paddle pop sticks, available from some newsagents, bamboo skewers (remove the pointed end) or even swirly plastic straws.

6

THE CAKE

• For each recipe, we have suggested a type of cake to suit the style of cake pop. Feel free to choose your own, but avoid anything too dry or light in texture. Varieties that work well are firm-textured butter, coconut, mud or fruit cakes. Leftover Christmas cakes and puddings work well too, as they're usually moist.

• To keep the preparation time to a minimum, we have mostly used shop-bought cakes. If you'd like to make your own, we've included four recipes (see pages 10 & 11).

• Discard any icing or filling unless specified, then crumble the cake with your hands into a large bowl. Pack it firmly into metric cup measures.

• As some cakes will differ in moisture content and texture, you may find that your cake crumbs weigh or compress differently to ours when measuring and rolling the ball shapes.

This may give you a different number of cake pops. Simply adjust the size of the cake pops if needed, or you may find you have extras.

• The freezer is a great help when preparing cake pops, as it chills and firms the mixture quickly. You can refrigerate cake pops instead if you don't have the freezer space, just allow more time.

DECORATING

• For most of the coatings we used compound chocolate buds or "Melts". These are much easier to work with than good quality eating chocolate, and the cake pops will keep their shape at room temperature.

• Note that white chocolate is a creamy yellow colour; if you want a white coating, you will need to purchase Candy Melts (different to chocolate Melts) from cake decorating suppliers. Candy Melts are also available in colours.

• When tinting white chocolate, remember that because you are starting with a cream-coloured base, the resulting colour may not be true. An example is rose pink colouring – it will turn a salmon pink colour when added to white chocolate. If you need to match a particular colour, use Candy Melts.

• We recommend using paste food colourings. Add just a little at a time.

• There are products available from cake decorating suppliers that help to thin chocolate and stabilise it when tinting, making dipping easier.

• If working with a large number of cake pops, take one batch at a time out of the freezer or fridge.

• You may need to re-melt the chocolate every now and again if it begins to thicken.

STORING

• Most cake pops can be made at least two days before the party.

• Store cake pops at a cool, dry room temperature. If the weather is humid, you may need to refrigerate them.

• Most cake pops will be firm enough, once set, to place lying down, in a single layer, in an airtight container. This makes them easy to store and transport.

• If you find the cake pops are a little soft, keep them standing up in styrofoam or egg cartons and cover them with an upturned box or container to keep them dust-free.

• See our tips for wrapping and presenting your pops on page 118.

Icing recipes

BUTTERCREAM

125g (4 ounces) butter, softened

1½ cups (240g) icing
(confectioners') sugar

2 tablespoons milk

1 Beat butter (and any flavouring, if using)
in a small narrow bowl with an electric
mixer until as white as possible.
2 Gradually beat in half the sifted icing
sugar, then milk, then the remaining sifted
icing sugar.
3 Beat until the buttercream is smooth and
spreadable. Keep scraping down the side of
the bowl while beating.

TIP Beating the butter until it whitens
will give you better results when colouring
your buttercream.

ROYAL ICING

1½ cups (240g) pure icing
(confectioners') sugar, approximately

1 egg white

¼ teaspoon strained lemon juice

1 Sift icing sugar through a fine sieve.
2 Lightly beat egg white in a small bowl
with an electric mixer until mixture is just
broken up – don't whip into peaks.
3 Beat in the icing sugar, one tablespoon
at a time, until the icing reaches a soft,
spoonable consistency.
4 Mix in the juice using a wooden spoon.
Cover surface of icing with plastic wrap to
keep airtight.

TIPS If you want to make small amounts
of royal icing, use a teaspoon of lightly
beaten egg white, then stir in enough icing
sugar to make the required consistency.
You can buy a royal icing mix from some
supermarkets and cake decorating suppliers
– this works well and is convenient to
use, especially if only small amounts are
required. Royal icing will keep at a cool room
temperature for several days. Beat with a
wooden spoon to bring icing back to the
required consistency. If you need to adjust
the consistency further, add a little more
icing sugar or lemon juice.

Cake recipes

BUTTER CAKE

125g (4 ounces) butter, softened

1 teaspoon vanilla extract

¾ cup (165g) caster (superfine) sugar

2 eggs

1½ cups (225g) self-raising flour

½ cup (125ml) milk

1 Preheat oven to 180°C/350°F. Grease a 20cm x 30cm (8-inch x 12-inch) rectangular slice pan; line base with baking paper, extending paper 5cm (2 inches) over long sides.
2 Beat butter, extract and sugar in a small bowl with an electric mixer until light and fluffy. Beat in eggs, one at a time. Transfer mixture to a large bowl; stir in sifted flour and milk, in two batches. Spread mixture into the pan.
3 Bake cake about 25 minutes. Stand cake in pan 2 minutes before turning, top-side up, onto a wire rack to cool.

WHITE CHOCOLATE MUD CAKE

150g (4½ ounces) unsalted butter, chopped coarsely

150g (4½ ounces) white eating chocolate, chopped coarsely

¾ cup (165g) caster (superfine) sugar

½ cup (125ml) milk

¾ cup (110g) plain (all-purpose) flour

¾ cup (110g) self-raising flour

2 eggs, beaten lightly

1 Preheat oven to 160°C/325°F. Grease a 20cm x 30cm (8-inch x 12-inch) rectangular slice pan; line base with baking paper, extending paper 5cm (2 inches) over long sides.
2 Stir butter, chocolate, sugar and milk in a medium saucepan over low heat until smooth. Transfer mixture to a medium bowl; cool 10 minutes. Whisk in sifted flours, then egg. Spread mixture into the pan.
3 Bake cake about 25 minutes. Stand cake in pan 2 minutes before turning, top-side up, onto a wire rack to cool.

CARAMEL MUD CAKE

150g (4½ ounces) unsalted butter, chopped coarsely

150g (4½ ounces) white eating chocolate, chopped coarsely

¾ cup (165g) firmly packed dark brown sugar

½ cup (125ml) milk

1½ tablespoons golden syrup or treacle

¾ cup (110g) plain (all-purpose) flour

¾ cup (110g) self-raising flour

2 eggs, beaten lightly

1 Preheat oven to 160°C/325°F. Grease a 20cm x 30cm (8-inch x 12-inch) rectangular slice pan; line base with baking paper, extending paper 5cm (2 inches) over long sides.
2 Stir butter, white chocolate, sugar, milk and syrup in a medium saucepan over low heat until smooth. Transfer mixture to a medium heatproof bowl; cool 10 minutes. Whisk in sifted flours, then egg. Spread mixture into the pan.
3 Bake cake about 25 minutes. Stand cake in pan 2 minutes before turning, top-side up, onto a wire rack to cool.

COCONUT CAKE

150g (4½ ounces) butter, softened

1 teaspoon coconut essence (extract)

1¼ cups (275g) caster (superfine) sugar

1 cup (250ml) coconut cream

1⅓ cups (200g) self-raising flour

4 egg whites

1 Preheat oven to 160°C/325°F. Grease a 20cm x 30cm (8-inch x 12-inch) rectangular slice pan; line base with baking paper, extending paper 5cm (2 inches) over long sides.
2 Beat butter, essence and sugar in a small bowl with an electric mixer until light and fluffy. Transfer mixture to a large bowl; stir in coconut cream and sifted flour, in two batches.
3 Beat egg whites in a clean small bowl with an electric mixer until soft peaks form. Fold egg whites into coconut mixture, in two batches. Spread mixture into the pan.
4 Bake cake about 30 minutes. Cool cake in pan.

decorations

12

Decorations

Some of these little sweets are from cake decorating suppliers, but most you'll find at the supermarket. Shop around and don't be afraid to use your imagination.

KIDS' *Cake Pops*

Here are some fabulous and fun ideas that your kids will love. There are lions, daisies, coconut & raspberry jellies, clowns and mini doughnut pops to make. These bite-sized treats not only look great, they taste fantastic, and are super-easy to eat.

BUILDING BLOCKS

4 cups (680g)
firmly packed butter
cake crumbs

⅓ cup (100g) ready-
made vanilla frosting

375g (12 ounces) white
chocolate Melts

24 lollipop or
paddle pop sticks

1 quantity royal icing
(see page 9)

pink, yellow and blue
food colouring

1 Line base and sides of a 20cm (8-inch) square cake pan with baking paper. Using a fork, combine cake crumbs and frosting in a medium bowl. Press mixture into the pan. Freeze 1 hour or refrigerate 3 hours or overnight, until firm. Lift mixture from pan; cut into 4cm x 4cm (1½-inch x 1½-inch) cubes.

2 Stir chocolate in a medium heatproof bowl over a medium saucepan of simmering water until smooth (don't let water touch base of bowl). Pour into a heatproof jug.

3 Dip the end of one stick into the chocolate, then push it about halfway into a cube of cake. Place on a baking paper-lined tray. Repeat with remaining sticks and cubes of cake. Place tray in the freezer for about 5 minutes to set.

4 Dip one cake pop into the chocolate, rocking back and forth to coat; don't swirl the pop, or it'll break. Allow excess to drip back into the jug. Stand cake pop upright in a styrofoam block (see page 6) until set. Repeat with remaining cake pops. Re-melt chocolate as necessary.

5 Divide royal icing between three small bowls; tint pale pink, yellow and blue. Cover surface of icings with plastic wrap to keep them airtight. Spoon pink icing into a small piping bag fitted with a 3mm (⅛-inch) tube. Pipe borders on each side of eight cubes to define edges; pipe letters inside the borders. Repeat with yellow and blue icing (in clean piping bags) and remaining cubes. Stand upright until set.

prep + cook time 1 hour 20 minutes (+ freezing & standing)
makes 24
store in an airtight container at a cool room temperature until ready to serve. Cake pops will keep for up to a week.

kids' cake pops

TIPS You'll have one leftover cube of cake – practise your piping on this if you like. Use white Candy Melts in place of chocolate Melts for an extra-white finish (see page 7).

BABY RATTLES

4 cups (680g)
firmly packed butter
cake crumbs

½ quantity
buttercream (see page 9)

375g (12 ounces)
white chocolate Melts

30 lollipop sticks or
bamboo skewers

30 striped
drinking straws

½ quantity royal
icing (see page 9)

blue, pink and yellow
food colouring

1 Using a fork, combine cake crumbs and about ½ cup of the buttercream in a medium bowl, until ingredients come together.
2 Shape level tablespoons of the mixture into balls, squeezing firmly. Place balls on a baking paper-lined tray; freeze 1 hour or refrigerate 3 hours or overnight, until firm.
3 Stir chocolate in a medium heatproof bowl over a medium saucepan of simmering water until smooth (don't let water touch base of bowl). Pour into a heatproof jug.
4 Dip the end of one stick into the chocolate, then push it about halfway into a ball of cake. Return to tray. Repeat with remaining sticks and balls of cake. Place tray in the freezer for about 5 minutes to set.
5 Dip one cake pop into the chocolate, rocking back and forth to coat; don't swirl the pop, or it'll break. Allow excess chocolate to drip back into the jug. Slide a straw over the stick, pushing it up into the chocolate. Stand cake pop upright in a styrofoam block (see page 6) until set. Repeat with remaining cake pops. Re-melt chocolate as necessary.
6 Divide royal icing into three small bowls; tint pale blue, pink and yellow. Cover surface of icings with plastic wrap to keep them airtight.
7 Spoon blue icing into a small paper piping bag; snip a tiny tip from the end. Pipe spirals on top of 10 of the cake pops, turning sticks in the styrofoam as you pipe. Repeat with pink and yellow icing (in clean piping bags) and remaining cake pops. Stand upright until set.
prep + cook time 1 hour 20 minutes (+ freezing & standing)
makes 30 **tip** See pages 120 & 121 for more information on piping chocolate.
store in an airtight container at a cool room temperature until ready to serve. Cake pops will keep for up to a week.

POSSUMS

4 cups (720g) firmly packed chocolate madeira cake crumbs

⅓ cup (100g) ready-made rich chocolate fudge frosting

375g (12 ounces) white chocolate Melts

28 x 15cm (6-inch) bamboo skewers

150g (4½ ounces) white chocolate Melts, extra

brown food colouring

¼ cup white sprinkles

168 x 1.5cm (¾-inch) lengths vermicelli noodles

4 pink musk or fruit sticks, sliced thinly

56 pink mini mallows

½ quantity royal icing (see page 9)

black food colouring

28 brown jumbo chenille sticks or pipe cleaners

1 Using a fork, combine cake crumbs and frosting in a medium bowl. Shape level tablespoons of mixture into balls, squeezing firmly. Place balls on a baking paper-lined tray; freeze 1 hour or refrigerate 3 hours or overnight, until firm.

2 Stir chocolate in a medium heatproof bowl over a medium saucepan of simmering water until smooth (don't let water touch base of bowl). Pour into a heatproof jug.

3 Dip the end of one skewer into the chocolate then push it about halfway into a ball of cake. Return to tray. Repeat with remaining skewers and balls of cake. Place tray in the freezer for about 5 minutes to set.

4 Dip one cake pop into the chocolate, rocking back and forth to coat; don't swirl the pop, or it'll break. Allow excess chocolate to drip back into the jug. Stand cake pop upright in a styrofoam block (see page 6) until set. Repeat with remaining cake pops. Re-melt chocolate as necessary.

5 Stir extra chocolate in a medium heatproof bowl over a medium saucepan of simmering water until smooth (don't let water touch base of bowl). Tint chocolate pale brown. Half-dip the pops into brown chocolate; scatter with sprinkles. Stand pops upright until set.

6 To make whiskers, attach six vermicelli pieces to the white side of each pop with a little of the remaining white chocolate. Top each with a musk stick slice for a nose. To make ears, flatten mallows with a rolling pin then secure two on each pop with a little white chocolate. Tint royal icing black; spoon into a small piping bag fitted with a 3mm (⅛-inch) tube. Pipe eyes onto pops. Stand upright until set.

7 Twist chenille sticks around skewers.

prep + cook time 1 hour 20 minutes (+ freezing & standing)
makes 28

TIP Possums without eyes can be made up to two days ahead. Store in an airtight container. Pipe eyes on the day of serving.

Buzzing yellow
HONEY BEES

4 cups (680g)
firmly packed butter
cake crumbs

⅓ cup (100g) ready-
made vanilla frosting

375g (12 ounces)
white chocolate Melts

yellow food colouring

18 lollipop or
paddle pop sticks

1 quantity royal icing
(see page 9)

black food colouring

36 white pieces (10g)
Milo Duo cereal

1 Using a fork, combine cake crumbs and frosting in a medium bowl. Shape level tablespoons of mixture into teardrop shapes, squeezing firmly. Place on a baking paper-lined tray; freeze 1 hour or refrigerate 3 hours or overnight, until firm.

2 Stir chocolate in a medium heatproof bowl over a medium saucepan of simmering water until smooth (don't let water touch base of bowl). Tint chocolate pale yellow. Pour into a heatproof jug.

3 Dip the end of one stick into the chocolate, then push it about halfway into a piece of cake. Return to tray. Repeat with remaining sticks and cakes. Place tray in the freezer for about 5 minutes to set.

4 Dip one cake pop into the chocolate, rocking back and forth to coat; don't swirl the pop, or it'll break. Allow excess chocolate to drip back into the jug. Stand cake pop upright in a styrofoam block (see page 6) until set. Repeat with remaining cake pops. Re-melt chocolate as necessary.

5 Tint royal icing black. Spoon icing into a small piping bag fitted with a 3mm (⅛-inch) tube. Pipe stripes, eyes and mouths onto bees. For the wings, secure two cereal pieces onto each bee with a little icing. Stand pops upright until set.

prep + cook time 1 hour 15 minutes (+ freezing & standing)
makes 18
store in an airtight container at a cool room temperature until ready to serve. Cake pops will keep for up to a week. Pipe stripes, eyes and mouths on the day of serving.

TIP Use yellow Candy Melts in place of tinted chocolate Melts if you like (see page 7).

Friendly
LITTLE LIONS

2½ cups (400g) firmly packed chocolate mud cake crumbs

½ cup (150g) ready-made milk chocolate frosting

375g (12 ounces) white chocolate Melts

orange food colouring

22 lollipop or paddle pop sticks

3 orange fruit sticks (10g)

22 brown Smarties (25g)

88 yellow Smarties (90g)

66 orange Smarties (65g)

66 red Smarties (65g)

132 x 2.5cm (1-inch) lengths vermicelli noodles

¼ quantity royal icing (see page 9)

black food colouring

1 Combine cake crumbs and frosting in a medium bowl. Using wet hands, shape level tablespoons of mixture into balls, squeezing firmly. Place on a baking paper-lined tray; freeze 1 hour or refrigerate 3 hours or overnight, until firm.

2 Melt white chocolate in a medium heatproof bowl over a medium saucepan of simmering water until smooth (don't let water touch base of bowl); tint chocolate pale orange. Pour into a heatproof jug.

3 Dip the end of one stick into chocolate, then push it about halfway into a ball of cake. Return to tray. Repeat with remaining sticks and balls of cake. Place tray in the freezer for about 5 minutes to set.

4 Meanwhile, cut 22 small triangles from fruit sticks for noses. Cut brown Smarties in half; attach to the top of pops with a little of the chocolate to make ears. Stand upright until set.

5 Dip one cake pop into the chocolate, covering the ears too, rocking back and forth to coat; don't swirl the pop, or it'll break. Allow excess chocolate to drip back into the jug. Stand upright in a styrofoam block (see page 6) until set. Repeat with remaining cake pops. Re-melt chocolate as necessary.

6 Cut an edge from each of the remaining Smarties; attach them to pops with a little chocolate for the mane. To make whiskers, attach six vermicelli pieces to each pop; top with fruit stick triangles for a nose. Stand pops upright until set.

7 Tint royal icing black. Spoon icing into a small piping bag fitted with a 3mm (⅛-inch) tube. Pipe on eyes and mouths.

prep + cook time 1 hour (+ freezing & standing)
makes 22 store in an airtight container at a cool room temperature until ready to serve. Cake pops will keep for up to a week. Pipe eyes and mouths on the day of serving. Don't refrigerate, as colouring on Smarties will run.

TIPS You'll need about 100g (3 ounces) noodles. Buy about 500g (1 pound) Smarties to get the colours we've used, or choose your own colours.

Lemon yellow
SMILEY FACES

4 cups (720g) firmly packed madeira cake crumbs

2 tablespoons finely grated lemon rind

1 tablespoon lemon juice

¼ cup (75g) ready-made vanilla frosting

275g (9 ounces) white chocolate Melts

yellow food colouring

18 lollipop or paddle pop sticks

¼ quantity royal icing (page 9)

black food colouring

1 Using a fork, combine cake crumbs, rind, juice and frosting in a medium bowl. Press level tablespoons of the mixture into a 5cm (2-inch) round cutter; round the edges with your fingers. Place rounds on a baking paper-lined tray; freeze 1 hour or refrigerate 3 hours or overnight, until firm.

2 Stir chocolate in a medium heatproof bowl over a medium saucepan of simmering water until smooth (don't let water touch base of bowl). Tint chocolate yellow; pour into a heatproof jug.

3 Dip the end of one stick into the chocolate, then push it about halfway into a round of cake. Return to tray. Repeat with remaining sticks and rounds of cake. Place tray in the freezer for about 5 minutes to set.

4 Dip one cake pop into the chocolate, rocking back and forth to coat; don't swirl the pop, or it'll break. Allow excess chocolate to drip back into the jug. Stand cake pop upright in a styrofoam block (see page 6) until set. Repeat with remaining cake pops. Re-melt chocolate as necessary.

5 Tint royal icing black. Spoon icing into a small piping bag fitted with a 3mm (⅛-inch) tube; pipe eyes and mouths onto rounds. Stand pops upright until set.

prep + cook time 1 hour (+ freezing & standing)

makes 18

store in an airtight container at a cool room temperature until ready to serve. Cake pops will keep for up to a week. Pipe eyes and mouths on the day of serving.

TIP Use yellow Candy Melts in place of tinted chocolate Melts if you like (see page 7).

Crazy colourful
STRAW POPS

4 cups (680g)
firmly packed butter
cake crumbs

⅓ cup (100g)
ready-made rich
chocolate fudge frosting

375g (12 ounces)
white chocolate Melts

----

28 decorative
drinking straws

1¼ cups (275g) coloured
sprinkles (we used
¼ cup each of dark
blue, light blue, orange,
pink and yellow)

----

1 Using a fork, combine cake crumbs and frosting in a medium bowl. Shape level tablespoons of mixture into balls, squeezing firmly. Place balls on a baking paper-lined tray; freeze 1 hour or refrigerate 3 hours or overnight, until firm.

2 Stir chocolate in a medium heatproof bowl over a medium saucepan of simmering water until smooth (don't let water touch base of bowl). Pour into a heatproof jug.

3 Dip the curly end of one straw into the chocolate, then push the straw about halfway into a ball of cake. Return to tray. Repeat with remaining straws and balls of cake. Place in the freezer for about 5 minutes to set.

4 Decorate about four cake pops at a time. Dip a pop into the chocolate, rocking back and forth to coat; don't swirl the pop, or it'll break. Allow excess chocolate to drip back into the jug. Stand cake pop upright in a styrofoam block (see page 6) until almost set. Place sprinkles in small bowls. Before chocolate completely sets, dip cake pop in sprinkles, turning to cover surface. Stand upright until set. Repeat with remaining cake pops. Re-melt chocolate as necessary.

prep + cook time 40 minutes (+ freezing & standing)
makes 28
store in an airtight container at a cool room temperature until ready to serve. Cake pops will keep for up to a week.

Baby blue
CAKE POPS

4 cups (680g)
firmly packed butter
cake crumbs

⅓ cup (100g) ready-
made vanilla frosting

375g (12 ounces)
white chocolate Melts

32 lollipop or paddle
pop sticks

100g (3 ounces) white
chocolate Melts, extra

blue food colouring

⅓ cup (70g) blue, green
and orange sprinkles

1 Using a fork, combine cake crumbs and frosting in a medium bowl. Shape level tablespoons of mixture into balls, squeezing firmly. Place balls on a baking paper-lined tray; freeze 1 hour or refrigerate 3 hours or overnight, until firm.
2 Stir chocolate in a medium heatproof bowl over a medium saucepan of simmering water until smooth (don't let water touch base of bowl). Pour into a heatproof jug.
3 Dip the end of one stick into the chocolate, push it about halfway into a ball of cake. Return to tray. Repeat with remaining sticks and balls of cake. Place in the freezer for about 5 minutes to set.
4 Dip one cake pop into the chocolate, rocking back and forth to coat; don't swirl the pop, or it'll break. Allow excess chocolate to drip back into the jug. Stand pop upright in a styrofoam block (see page 6) until set. Repeat with remaining cake pops. Re-melt chocolate as necessary.
5 Stir extra chocolate in a medium heatproof bowl over a medium saucepan of simmering water until smooth (don't let water touch base of bowl). Tint chocolate pale blue. Pour into a heatproof jug.
6 Dip the top of a cake pop into the blue chocolate; scatter with sprinkles. Repeat with remaining pops, chocolate and sprinkles. Stand pops upright until set.
prep + cook time 50 minutes (+ freezing & standing)
makes 32
store in an airtight container at a cool room temperature until ready to serve. Cake pops will keep for up to a week.

TIP Use Candy Melts in place of tinted chocolate Melts for more accurate colours (see page 7).

Coconut & raspberry
JELLY POPS

4 cups (680g)
firmly packed butter
cake crumbs

⅓ cup (100g) ready-
made vanilla frosting

85g (3 ounces) raspberry
jelly crystals

50g (1½ ounces)
white chocolate Melts

30 lollipop sticks
or bamboo skewers

1 cup (80g)
desiccated coconut

30 coloured
drinking straws

1 Using a fork, combine cake crumbs and frosting in a medium bowl. Roll level tablespoons of mixture into balls. Place balls on a baking paper-lined tray, freeze 1 hour or refrigerate 3 hours or overnight, until firm.

2 Make jelly according to packet instructions; pour into a shallow baking pan. Refrigerate for about an hour or until jelly has thickened slightly.

3 Stir chocolate in a small heatproof bowl over a small saucepan of simmering water until smooth (don't let water touch base of bowl). Dip the end of one stick into the chocolate, then push it halfway into a ball of cake. Return to tray. Repeat with remaining sticks and balls of cake. Place in the freezer for about 5 minutes to set.

4 Transfer partially-set jelly to a small bowl or jug; place coconut in another small bowl. Dip one cake pop into jelly; rocking back and forth to coat; don't swirl the pop, or it'll break. Allow excess jelly to drip back into the jug. Dip pop in coconut to cover jelly completely. Stand cake pop upright in a styrofoam block (see page 6). Repeat with remaining cake pops, jelly and coconut. Refrigerate until set.

5 Carefully slide straws over sticks, pushing them up into pops until they feel secure.

prep + cook time 45 minutes (+ freezing & refrigeration)
makes 30
store in an airtight container in the refrigerator until ready to serve. Cake pops will keep for up to a week.

TIP You can use any flavoured jelly you wish.

Rainbow popcorn
MOON ROCKS

1¼ cups (220g) firmly packed madeira cake crumbs

1½ tablespoons apricot jam

300g (9½ ounces) white chocolate Melts

green food colouring

14 lollipop or paddle pop sticks

3 cups (35g) coloured sugared popcorn

1 Using a fork, combine cake crumbs and jam in a small bowl. Shape level tablespoons of mixture into balls, squeezing firmly. Place balls on a baking paper-lined tray; freeze 1 hour or refrigerate 3 hours or overnight, until firm.

2 Stir chocolate in a medium heatproof bowl over a medium saucepan of simmering water until smooth (don't let water touch base of bowl). Tint chocolate green. Pour into a heatproof jug.

3 Dip the end of one stick into the chocolate, then push it about halfway into a ball of cake. Return to tray. Repeat with remaining sticks and balls of cake. Place in the freezer for about 5 minutes to set.

4 Break popcorn into small pieces.

5 Dip one pop into the chocolate, rocking back and forth to coat; don't swirl the pop, or it'll break. Allow excess chocolate to drip back into the jug. Press on popcorn to cover surface. Stand cake pop upright in a styrofoam block (see page 6) until set. Repeat with remaining pops, chocolate and popcorn; re-melt chocolate as necessary.

prep + cook time 45 minutes (+ freezing & standing)

makes 14

store in an airtight container at a cool room temperature until ready to serve. Cake pops will keep for up to a week.

TIP Cake pops can be made at least two days before the party.

CIRCUS CLOWNS

1¼ cups (220g) firmly packed madeira cake crumbs

2 teaspoons strawberry jam

300g (9½ ounces) white chocolate Melts

10 lollipop or paddle pop sticks

10 mini ice-cream cones

2 tablespoons hundreds and thousands

10 jaffas

30cm (12-inch) length strawberry licorice bootlaces

20 pink mini M&M'S

¼ quantity royal icing (page 9)

black food colouring

28g (1 ounce) pink Nerds

1 Using a fork, combine cake crumbs and jam in a small bowl. Shape level tablespoons of mixture into balls, squeezing firmly. Place balls on a baking paper-lined tray; freeze 1 hour or refrigerate 3 hours or overnight, until firm.

2 Stir chocolate in a medium heatproof bowl over a medium saucepan of simmering water until smooth (don't let water touch base of bowl). Pour into a heatproof jug.

3 Dip the end of one stick into chocolate, then push it about halfway into a ball of cake. Return to tray. Repeat with remaining sticks and balls of cake. Place in the freezer for about 5 minutes to set.

4 Dip a cake pop into the chocolate, rocking back and forth to coat; don't swirl the pop, or it'll break. Allow excess chocolate to drip back into the jug. Stand cake pop upright in a styrofoam block (see page 6) until set. Repeat with remaining cake pops. Re-melt chocolate as necessary.

5 Carefully trim 4.5cm (1¾ inches) from the wide end of the cones, discard trimmings. Dip the edge and tip of one (now smaller) cone in chocolate then dip in hundreds and thousands. Place cone on top of a cake pop to make the clown's hat. Hold in place for about a minute or until just set. Repeat with remaining cones, chocolate and hundreds and thousands. Stand upright until set.

6 Using a little melted chocolate, secure jaffa noses onto the clowns. Cut licorice into 12 x 2cm (¾-inch) lengths; secure a piece onto each clown to form the mouth. Secure two mini M&M's on each clown for the rosy cheeks.

7 Tint royal icing black. Spoon icing into a piping bag fitted with a 3mm (⅛-inch) tube. Pipe crosses for the eyes. To make hair, secure Nerds near the cone using a little more chocolate.

prep + cook time 1 hour (+ freezing & standing)
makes 10 **store** in an airtight container at a cool room temperature until ready to serve. Don't refrigerate. Pipe eyes on the day of serving. Cake pops will keep for up to a week.

TIP Use white Candy Melts in place of chocolate Melts for an extra-white finish (see page 7).

Glazed caramel
DOUGHNUTS

3½ cups (560g) firmly packed caramel mud cake crumbs

- - - - - - - - - - - - - - - - - - -

1 tablespoon ready-made rich chocolate fudge frosting

- - - - - - - - - - - - - - - - - - -

100g (3 ounces) dark (semi-sweet) chocolate Melts

- - - - - - - - - - - - - - - - - - -

100g (3 ounces) pink Candy Melts (see page 7)

- - - - - - - - - - - - - - - - - - -

¼ cup (60g) hundreds and thousands

- - - - - - - - - - - - - - - - - - -

16 lollipop or paddle pop sticks

- - - - - - - - - - - - - - - - - - -

1 Using a fork, combine cake crumbs and frosting in a medium bowl. Using wet hands, shape level tablespoons of mixture into balls, squeezing firmly. Press mixture into a 4.5cm (1¾-inch) cutter to form a round. Using the end of a wooden spoon, press a hole in the centre of each round. Carefully transfer rings to a baking paper-lined tray; freeze 1 hour or refrigerate 3 hours or overnight, until firm.

2 Stir dark chocolate in a medium heatproof bowl over a medium saucepan of simmering water until smooth (don't let water touch base of bowl). Repeat for Candy Melts.

3 Spoon a small amount of the melted chocolate or Candy Melts over rings; scatter with hundreds and thousands. Return to trays. Stand until completely set. Insert sticks.

prep + cook time 45 minutes (+ freezing & standing)

makes 16

tip It's fine to use white chocolate Melts tinted with pink food colouring, in place of the pink Candy Melts.

store in an airtight container at a cool room temperature until ready to serve. Cake pops will keep for up to a week.

Swirly marble
LOLLIPOPS

4 cups (680g) firmly packed orange cake crumbs

⅓ cup (100g) ready-made vanilla frosting

425g (13½ ounces) white chocolate Melts

pink food colouring

38 lollipop sticks or bamboo skewers

38 coloured drinking straws

1 Using a fork, combine cake crumbs and frosting in a medium bowl. Shape 3 level teaspoons of mixture into balls, squeezing firmly. Place balls on a baking paper-lined tray; freeze 1 hour, or refrigerate 3 hours or overnight, until firm.

2 Stir chocolate in a medium heatproof bowl over a medium saucepan of simmering water until smooth (don't let water touch base of bowl). Transfer two-thirds of the chocolate into a small bowl; tint remaining chocolate pale pink.

3 Dip the end of one stick into the chocolate, then push it about halfway into a ball of cake. Return to tray. Repeat with remaining sticks and balls of cake. Place in the freezer for about 5 minutes to set.

4 Dip one cake pop into the white chocolate, rocking back and forth to coat; don't swirl the pop, or it'll break. Allow excess chocolate to drip back into the jug. While cake pop is still wet, drizzle a little of the pink chocolate over the top, swirling pop until smooth. Slide a straw over the stick, pushing it up into the chocolate. Stand cake pop upright in a styrofoam block (see page 6) until set. Repeat with remaining cake pops. Re-melt chocolate as necessary.

prep + cook time 1 hour (+ freezing & standing)

makes 38

store in an airtight container at a cool room temperature until ready to serve. Cake pops will keep for up to a week.

TIP Use white Candy Melts in place of chocolate Melts for an extra-white finish (see page 7).

DAISIES

40g (1½ ounces)
cream cheese, softened

15g (½ ounce) butter,
softened

½ teaspoon
vanilla extract

⅔ cup (110g) icing
(confectioners') sugar

2½ cups (450g)
firmly packed madeira
cake crumbs

375g (12 ounces)
white chocolate Melts

20 lollipop or paddle
pop sticks

120 (50g) white
mini mallows

20 mini yellow M&M's

10 mint leaf lollies, halved

1 Beat cream cheese, butter and extract in a small bowl with an electric mixer until light and fluffy; gradually beat in sifted icing sugar.

2 Using a fork, combine cream cheese mixture and crumbs in a medium bowl. Using wet hands, roll level tablespoons of mixture into balls, squeezing firmly. Place balls on a baking paper-lined tray. Freeze 1 hour, or refrigerate 3 hours or overnight, until firm.

3 Melt chocolate in a medium heatproof bowl over a medium saucepan of simmering water (don't let water touch base of bowl). Transfer to a heatproof jug.

4 Dip the end of one stick into chocolate, then push it about halfway into a ball of cake. Return to tray. Repeat with remaining sticks and balls of cake. Place tray in the freezer for about 5 minutes to set.

5 Using a rolling pin, flatten mallows.

6 Decorate about four cake pops at a time. Dip a pop into the chocolate, rocking back and forth to coat; don't swirl the pop, or it'll break. Allow excess chocolate to drip back into the jug. Stand cake pop upright in a styrofoam block (see page 6). Before chocolate on pop completely sets, decorate with mallows and an M&M. Stand upright until set. Repeat with remaining cake pops. Re-melt chocolate as necessary.

7 Slide mint leaves onto sticks.

prep + cook time 1 hour (+ freezing & standing)
makes 20
store cake pops in an airtight container at a cool room temperature until ready to serve. They will keep for up to 2 days. Don't refrigerate.

Stained glass
CAKE POPS

1⅓ cups (230g) firmly packed butter cake crumbs

1½ tablespoons apricot jam

300g (9½ ounces) white chocolate Melts

18 lollipop or paddle pop sticks

200g (5½ ounces) jubes, sliced thinly

1 Using a fork, combine cake crumbs and jam in a medium bowl. Shape 2 level teaspoons of mixture into balls, squeezing firmly. Place on a baking paper-lined tray; freeze 1 hour or refrigerate 3 hours or overnight, until firm.

2 Stir chocolate in a medium heatproof bowl over a medium saucepan of simmering water until smooth (don't let water touch base of bowl). Transfer to a heatproof jug.

3 Dip the end of one stick into the chocolate, then push it about halfway into a ball of cake. Return to tray. Repeat with remaining sticks and balls of cake. Place tray in the freezer for about 5 minutes to set.

4 Decorate about four cake pops at a time. Dip a pop into the chocolate, rocking back and forth to coat; don't swirl the pop, or it'll break. Allow excess chocolate to drip back into the jug. Stand cake pop upright in a styrofoam block (see page 6). Before chocolate on pop completely sets, cover with jube slices. Stand upright until set. Repeat with remaining cake pops. Re-melt chocolate as necessary.

prep + cook time 1½ hours (+ freezing & standing)
makes 18
store cake pops in an airtight container at a cool room temperature until ready to serve. They will keep for up to a week.

TIPS Any small jubes or jelly sweets can be used. Use lightly oiled scissors to cut the jubes.

WEDDING
Cake Pops

Cake pops are perfect for wedding celebrations. You can use them with your place cards, wedding favours, or as a great alternative to a slice of cake. They are a lovely way to personalise your wedding.

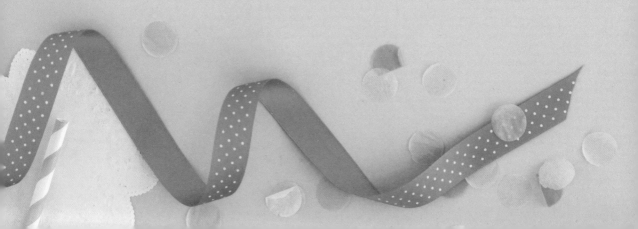

WEDDING CAKES

3 cups (500g) firmly packed butter cake crumbs

½ quantity buttercream (see page 9)

750g (1½ pounds) white Candy Melts (see page 7)

18 long thin toothpicks

9 lollipop or paddle pop sticks

½ quantity royal icing (see page 9)

1 packet 2mm (⅛-inch) white sugar pearls

9 white sugar flowers

1 Grease and line a deep 19cm (8-inch) square cake pan. Using a fork, combine cake crumbs and ⅓ cup of the buttercream in a medium bowl. Press mixture evenly into the pan; cover and freeze 1 hour or refrigerate 3 hours or overnight, until firm.

2 Stir Candy Melts in a medium heatproof bowl over a medium saucepan of simmering water until smooth (don't let water touch base of bowl). Pour into a heatproof jug.

3 Cut 9 x 5cm (2-inch) rounds, 9 x 3.5cm (1½-inch) rounds and 9 x 2.5cm (1-inch) rounds from cake mixture (see tip).

4 Dip the end of one toothpick into Candy Melts, then push it about halfway into the middle of a 2.5cm round. Repeat with remaining toothpicks, 2.5cm rounds and 3.5cm rounds. Dip the end of a lollipop stick into Melts; push stick all the way through a 5cm round, extending stick about 4.5cm (1¾-inches) past the top of the cake. Repeat with remaining sticks and 5cm rounds. Freeze cakes 5 minutes to set.

5 Dip each round of cake into the Candy Melts, rocking back and forth to coat; don't swirl the rounds, or they'll break. Allow excess Melts to drip back into the jug. Stand rounds upright in a styrofoam block (see page 6) until set. Re-melt Candy Melts as necessary.

6 To assemble wedding cakes, scrape away any excess Candy Melts from toothpicks. Remove 3.5cm rounds from toothpicks, carefully push onto lollipop sticks, on top of the 5cm rounds. Repeat with 2.5cm rounds. Use a little of the re-melted Candy Melts to join tiers together.

7 Spoon royal icing into a small piping bag fitted with a 3mm (⅛-inch) tube. Working in small sections, pipe tiny dots around the base of 2.5cm and 3.5cm tiers; using tweezers, position pearls in wet icing. Repeat all the way around cakes. Secure flowers to cakes with a little royal icing.

prep + cook time 2 hours (+ freezing & standing)
makes 9

wedding cake pops

TIPS Cut out cake rounds as close together as possible. Squash and press remaining cake mixture together, freeze, and cut out more shapes, if necessary. See page 122 for more information on assembling the wedding cakes. Store cake pops in an airtight container at a cool room temperature until ready to serve. They will keep for up to a week.

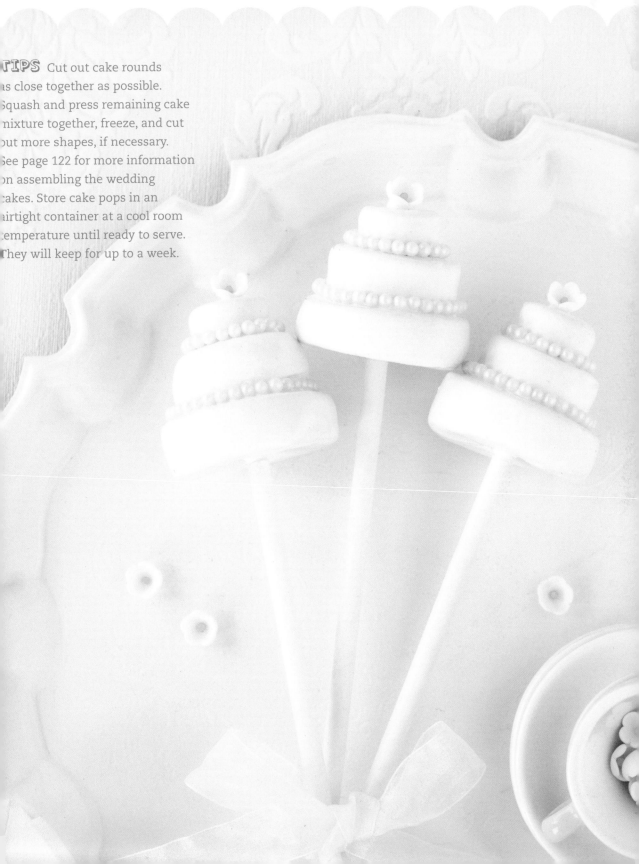

TOP HATS

2 cups (340g)
firmly packed butter
cake crumbs

½ quantity
buttercream (see page 9)

375g (12 ounces)
white chocolate Melts

black food colouring

9 lollipop or paddle
pop sticks

50g (1½ ounces)
ready-made white icing

cornflour (cornstarch)

½ quantity royal icing
(see page 9)

1 Grease and line a deep 15cm (6-inch) square cake pan. Using a fork, combine cake crumbs and ¼ cup of the buttercream in a medium bowl. Press mixture evenly into the pan; cover, freeze 1 hour or refrigerate 3 hours or overnight, until firm.

2 Stir chocolate in a medium heatproof bowl over a medium saucepan of simmering water until smooth (don't let water touch base of bowl); use black colouring to tint chocolate grey. Pour into a heatproof jug.

3 Use a 3cm (1¼-inch) cutter to cut 18 rounds from the cake crumb mixture (see tip). Join two rounds with a little of the chocolate. Repeat with remaining rounds.

4 Dip the end of one stick into the chocolate; push it through the rounds about halfway into the top round. Freeze cakes for about 5 minutes to set.

5 Dip one cake pop into the grey chocolate, rocking back and forth to coat; don't swirl the pop, or it'll break. Allow excess chocolate to drip back into the jug. Stand pop upright in a styrofoam block (see page 6) until set. Repeat with remaining cake pops. Re-melt chocolate as necessary.

6 To make brims for hats, re-melt chocolate; spread chocolate, about 2mm (⅛-inch) thick, onto a sheet of baking paper. Stand 10 minutes or until almost set. Use a 5cm (2-inch) round cutter to cut 9 rounds from chocolate. Use a metal skewer to pierce a hole through the centre of the rounds (heat skewer if chocolate has hardened); thread brims onto sticks underneath cake. Secure with melted chocolate. Stand upright until set.

7 Knead ready-made icing on a surface dusted with cornflour until icing loses its stickiness. Roll icing on a surface dusted with cornflour until 2mm (⅛ inch) thick. Cut icing into 9 strips, measuring 1cm x 8cm (½ inch x 3¼ inches), or long enough to wrap around the hat. Secure bands to hats with a little royal icing.

prep + cook time 1 hour (+ freezing & standing)
makes 9

TIPS Cut out cake rounds as close together as possible. Squash and press remaining cake mixture together, freeze and cut out more shapes, if necessary. See page 122 for some more information on assembling the top hats. Store cake pops in an airtight container at a cool room temperature until ready to serve. They will keep for up to a week.

TOFFEE PUFF POPS

⅓ cup (80ml) water

40g (1½ ounces) butter, finely chopped

3 teaspoons caster (superfine) sugar

⅓ cup (50g) strong baker's flour

2 eggs

34 paddle pop sticks

crème pâtissière

1⅓ cups (330ml) milk

⅓ cup (75g) caster (superfine) sugar

1 teaspoon vanilla extract

2 tablespoons cornflour (cornstarch)

3 egg yolks

toffee

2 cups (440g) caster (superfine) sugar

1 cup (250ml) water

1 Make crème pâtissière.

2 Preheat oven to 220°C/425°F. Grease oven trays.

3 To make choux pastry, combine the water, butter and sugar in a small saucepan; bring to the boil. Add the flour, beat with a wooden spoon over heat until mixture comes away from the base of the pan. Transfer pastry to a medium bowl; beat in eggs, one at a time, until pastry becomes glossy.

4 Drop rounded teaspoons of pastry, about 5cm (2 inches) apart, onto trays.

5 Bake puffs 10 minutes. Reduce the oven to 180°C/350°F; bake about 15 minutes or until golden brown. Cut a small opening in the base of each puff; bake a further 10 minutes or until puffs are dry. Cool on trays.

6 Spoon crème pâtissière into a piping bag fitted with a 3mm (⅛-inch) plain tube; pipe crème pâtissière into puffs through the openings.

7 Make toffee.

8 Push one paddle pop stick into each puff. Working quickly, dip puffs in toffee; place on a baking paper-lined oven tray. Stand at room temperature until set. Serve in foil cases.

crème pâtissière Combine milk, sugar and extract in a small saucepan; bring to the boil. Meanwhile, combine cornflour and egg yolks in a medium heatproof bowl; gradually whisk in hot milk mixture. Return mixture to pan; stir over heat until custard boils and thickens. Cover surface of custard with plastic wrap; refrigerate 4 hours.

toffee Stir sugar and the water in a medium saucepan over heat, without boiling, until sugar dissolves. Bring to the boil; boil, uncovered, without stirring, until a small amount of toffee dropped into cold water sets hard and can be snapped with fingers.

prep + cook time 1 hour 30 minutes (+ refrigeration & standing) makes 34 store at a cool room temperature; don't refrigerate. Serve puff pops within 6 hours of making.

TIPS For more information on making toffee puff pops see page 123. When dipping the puff pops in toffee, tilt the pan of toffee to one side, so it's deep enough to completely coat the pops. Dip one end of each stick in toffee too, this will ensure the pops don't fall off the sticks.

Lemon
MERINGUE POPS

4 cups (680g)
firmly packed butter
cake crumbs

⅓ cup (100g)
ready-made
vanilla frosting

50g (1½ ounces)
white chocolate Melts

32 lollipop or
paddle pop sticks

⅓ cup (110g)
ready-made
lemon curd (butter)

1 cup (220g) white sugar

⅓ cup (80ml) water

2 egg whites

1 Using a fork, combine cake crumbs and frosting in a medium bowl. Roll level tablespoons of mixture into balls. Place balls on a baking paper-lined tray, freeze 1 hour or refrigerate 3 hours or overnight, until firm.
2 Stir chocolate in a small heatproof bowl over a small saucepan of simmering water (don't let water touch base of bowl). Pour into a heatproof jug.
3 Dip the end of one stick into the chocolate, then push it about halfway into a ball of cake. Return to tray. Repeat with remaining sticks and balls of cake. Freeze for about 5 minutes to set.
4 Using a sharp knife, cut one-third off the top of each cake pop to create a flat top; discard off-cuts. Stand cake pops upright in a styrofoam block (see page 6). Stir lemon curd in a small bowl with a fork until smooth. Spoon curd into a piping bag; pipe a small amount of curd onto the top of each cake pop. Return pops to the freezer for 1 hour.
5 Combine sugar and the water in a small saucepan; stir over medium heat, without boiling, until sugar dissolves. Bring to the boil. Reduce heat, simmer, uncovered, without stirring, until syrup reaches 115°C/240°F on a candy thermometer. When syrup reaches 115°C, start beating egg whites in a small bowl with an electric mixer until soft peaks form. While beating egg whites, bring sugar syrup to 121°C/250°F. With motor operating, gradually pour syrup into egg white in a thin steady stream; continue beating until mixture is thick, glossy and cooled to room temperature.
6 Dip each cake pop into meringue mixture, swirling to coat. Stand pops upright until meringue is dry to touch.
7 If you like, lightly brown meringue coating with a chef's blowtorch, holding it no more than 20cm (8 inches) away.
prep + cook time 45 minutes (+ freezing & standing)
makes 32

TIP Store cake pops at a cool room temperature until ready to serve. They will keep for up to 6 hours.

Turkish delight
BOUQUETS

40g (1½ ounces) cream cheese, softened

15g (½ ounce) butter, softened

⅔ cup (110g) icing (confectioners') sugar

½ teaspoon rosewater

2½ cups (450g) firmly packed madeira cake crumbs

100g (3 ounces) rose turkish delight, chopped finely

¼ cup (35g) unsalted, roasted, finely chopped pistachios

375g (12 ounces) white chocolate Melts

20 lollipop or paddle pop sticks

220g (7 ounces) sugar flowers

1 Beat cream cheese and butter in a small bowl with an electric mixer until light and fluffy; gradually beat in sifted icing sugar until combined. Beat in rosewater.

2 Stir in cake crumbs, turkish delight and nuts. Using wet hands, shape level tablespoons of the mixture into balls, squeezing firmly. Place balls on a baking paper-lined tray; freeze 1 hour or refrigerate 3 hours or overnight, until firm.

3 Stir chocolate in a medium heatproof bowl over a medium saucepan of simmering water until smooth (don't let water touch base of bowl). Pour into a heatproof jug.

4 Dip the end of one stick into the chocolate, then push it about halfway into a ball of cake. Return to tray. Repeat with remaining sticks and balls of cake. Place in the freezer for about 5 minutes to set.

5 Dip one cake pop into the chocolate, rocking back and forth to coat; don't swirl the pop, or it'll break. Allow excess chocolate to drip back into the jug. Stand pop upright in a styrofoam block (see page 6). Attach flowers to pop. If chocolate sets before all are attached, re-melt chocolate and use a little to attach remaining flowers. Stand upright until set. Repeat with remaining cake pops and flowers.

prep + cook time 1 hour 30 minutes (+ freezing & standing)
makes 20

store in an airtight container at a cool room temperature until ready to serve. Cake pops will keep for up to a day.

TIPS Use lightly oiled scissors to cut turkish delight. You will need about 35 sugar flowers per cake pop. Use white Candy Melts in place of chocolate Melts for an extra-white finish (see page 7).

COCONUT POPS

40g (1½ ounces) cream cheese, softened

15g (½ ounce) butter, softened

⅔ cup (110g) icing (confectioners') sugar

2 tablespoons coconut rum or coconut liqueur

2 teaspoons finely grated lime rind

4½ cups (450g) firmly packed sponge cake crumbs

375g (12 ounces) white chocolate Melts

20 lollipop or paddle pop sticks

1 cup (100g) moist coconut flakes

1 Beat cream cheese and butter in a small bowl with electric mixer until light and fluffy; gradually beat in sifted icing sugar.
2 Using a fork, combine cream cheese mixture, rum and rind into cake crumbs in a medium bowl. Using wet hands, shape rounded tablespoons of mixture into balls, squeezing firmly. Place balls on a baking paper-lined tray; freeze 1 hour or refrigerate 3 hours or overnight, until firm.
3 Stir chocolate in a medium heatproof bowl over a medium saucepan of simmering water until smooth (don't let base of bowl touch water). Pour into a heatproof jug.
4 Dip the end of one stick into the chocolate, then push it about halfway into a ball of cake. Return to tray. Repeat with remaining sticks and balls of cake. Place in the freezer for about 5 minutes to set.
5 Dip one cake pop into the chocolate, rocking back and forth to coat; don't swirl the pop, or it'll break. Allow excess chocolate to drip back into the jug. Stand pop upright in a styrofoam block (see page 6). When chocolate has almost set, press coconut flakes onto cake pop to cover. Stand upright to set. Repeat with remaining cake pops and coconut. Re-melt chocolate as necessary.

prep + cook time 1 hour (+ freezing & standing)
makes 20
store in the refrigerator until ready to serve. Cake pops will keep for up to a week.

wedding cake pops

TIP Use white Candy Melts in place of chocolate Melts for an extra-white finish (see page 7).

Mint chocolate
CAKE POPS

⅓ cup (80ml) thickened (heavy) cream

80g (2½ ounces) dark eating (semi-sweet) chocolate, chopped

½ teaspoon peppermint essence

2½ cups (400g) firmly packed chocolate mud cake crumbs

180g (5½ ounces) dark chocolate Melts

375g (12 ounces) white Candy Melts (see page 7)

green food colouring

27 lollipop or paddle pop sticks

1 Bring cream to the boil in a small saucepan; remove from heat. Add chopped chocolate and essence, stand 2 minutes; stir until smooth.

2 Stir chocolate mixture into cake crumbs in a medium bowl. Using wet hands, shape level tablespoons of the mixture into balls, squeezing firmly. Place balls on a baking paper-lined tray. Freeze 1 hour, or refrigerate 3 hours or overnight, until set.

3 Stir dark chocolate Melts in a medium heatproof bowl over a medium saucepan of simmering water until smooth (don't let base of bowl touch water). Transfer to a heatproof jug. Stir Candy Melts in a medium heatproof bowl as above; divide Melts between two heatproof jugs. Tint one pale green.

4 Dip the end of one stick into the chocolate, then push the stick about halfway into a ball of cake. Return to tray. Repeat with another 8 sticks, chocolate and balls of cake. Do the same with remaining sticks, balls of cake and green and white Candy Melts. Place tray in freezer for about 5 minutes to set.

5 Re-melt dark chocolate if necessary. Dip 9 of the cake pops, one at a time, into the chocolate; rocking back and forth to coat; don't swirl the pops, or they'll break. Allow excess chocolate to drip back into the jug. Stand pops upright in a styrofoam block (see page 6) until set. Repeat with green and white Candy Melts.

6 Spoon remaining chocolate and Melts into 3 piping bags fitted with 3mm (⅛-inch) tubes. Drizzle chocolate and Melts over balls as pictured. Stand at room temperature until set.

prep + cook time 1 hour 15 minutes (+ freezing & standing)
makes 27
store in an airtight container at a cool room temperature until ready to serve. Cake pops will keep for up to a week.

Rich chocolate
BROWNIE BOMBS

75g (2½ ounces) butter, chopped coarsely

100g (3 ounces) dark eating (semi-sweet) chocolate, chopped coarsely

⅓ cup (75g) caster (superfine) sugar

1 egg

⅔ cup (100g) plain (all-purpose) flour

2 tablespoons dark rum

375g (12 ounces) dark chocolate Melts

30 lollipop or paddle pop sticks

2 tablespoons (28g) Choc Pearls

1 Preheat oven to 180°C/350°F. Grease a deep 18cm (7¼-inch) square cake pan; line base and sides with baking paper.

2 Stir butter and chopped chocolate in a small saucepan over low heat until smooth; transfer to a medium bowl, cool 10 minutes.

3 Stir sugar, egg and flour into chocolate mixture. Spread into pan; bake about 20 minutes. Cool in pan.

4 Cut cake into large pieces; using a food processor, process cake with rum until mixture just comes together. Shape rounded teaspoons of the mixture into balls. Place on a baking paper-lined tray. Freeze 1 hour or refrigerate 3 hours or overnight, until firm.

5 Stir chocolate Melts in a medium heatproof bowl over a medium saucepan of simmering water until smooth (don't let water touch base of bowl). Pour into a heatproof jug.

6 Dip the end of one stick into the chocolate, then push it about halfway into a ball of cake. Return to tray. Repeat with remaining sticks and balls of cake. Place tray in the freezer for about 5 minutes to set.

7 Dip one cake pop into the chocolate, rocking back and forth to coat; don't swirl the pop, or it'll break. Allow excess chocolate to drip back into the jug. Stand on a baking paper-lined tray; sprinkle with Pearls before chocolate sets. Repeat with remaining cake pops and Pearls. Stand at room temperature until set. Serve in paper cases.

prep + cook time 1 hour (+ cooling, freezing & standing)
makes 30
store in an airtight container at a cool room temperature until ready to serve. Cake pops will keep for up to a week.

Pistachio
MACAROON POPS

⅓ cup (45g) unsalted roasted pistachios

3 egg whites

¼ cup (55g) caster (superfine) sugar

green food colouring

1¼ cups (200g) pure icing (confectioners') sugar

¾ cup (90g) ground almonds

3 sheets silver leaf

¼ cup (60ml) pouring cream

150g (5 ounces) white eating chocolate, chopped finely

16 lollipop or paddle pop sticks

1 Grease two oven trays; line with baking paper. Process pistachios until finely ground.

2 Beat egg whites in a small bowl with an electric mixer until soft peaks form. Add caster sugar and a few drops of colouring, beat until sugar dissolves; transfer mixture to a medium bowl. Fold in ¼ cup of the ground pistachios, sifted icing sugar and ground almonds, in two batches.

3 Spoon mixture into a piping bag fitted with 1cm (½-inch) plain tube. Pipe 4cm (1½-inch) rounds about 2.5cm (1 inch) apart onto the trays. Tap trays on bench so macaroons spread slightly. Stand about 30 minutes to 1 hour, or until macaroons feel dry to touch.

4 Meanwhile, preheat the oven to 150°C/300°F. Bake macaroons about 20 minutes or until firm to touch. Cool on trays.

5 Using a skewer, gently push small pieces of silver leaf onto macaroons, taking care not to touch leaf with hands.

6 Bring cream to the boil in a small saucepan, remove from heat; add chocolate, stir until smooth. Refrigerate 20 minutes or until spreadable, stirring every 5 minutes.

7 Sandwich macaroons with 1 teaspoon chocolate filling. Insert a stick about halfway into chocolate between macaroons; place on tray. Refrigerate until set.

8 Tie bows onto sticks before serving, if you like. You will need 3.5 metres (3.8 yards) of thin ribbon.

prep + cook time 1 hour (+ standing, cooling & refrigeration)
makes 16
store in the refrigerator until ready to serve. Macaroon pops will keep for up to 2 days.

TIPS Silver leaf, available from cake decorating stores, is delicate and fiddly to handle but worth the effort. See page 122 for more information on applying silver leaf. Macaroons without chocolate filling will keep in an airtight container for up to a week. Once joined, they will keep refrigerated for up to 2 days.

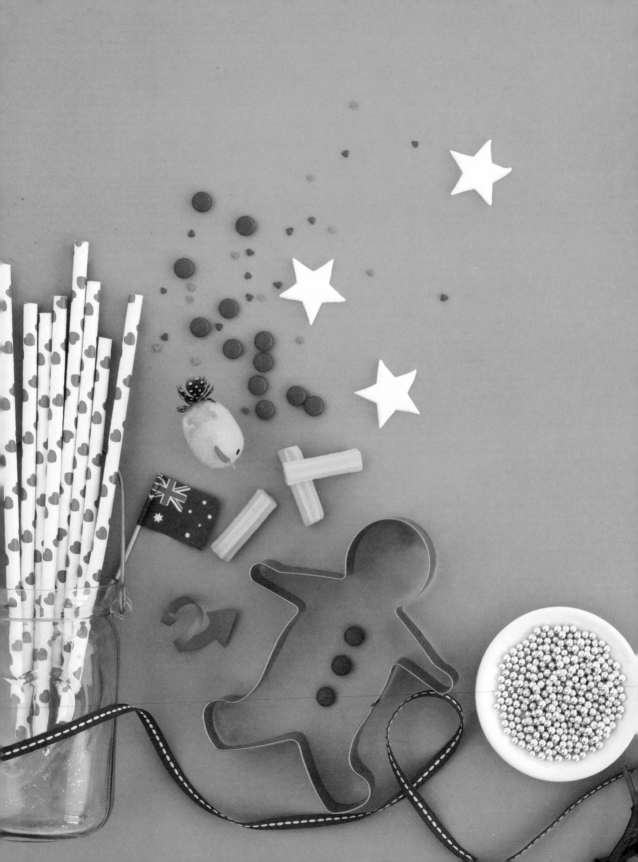

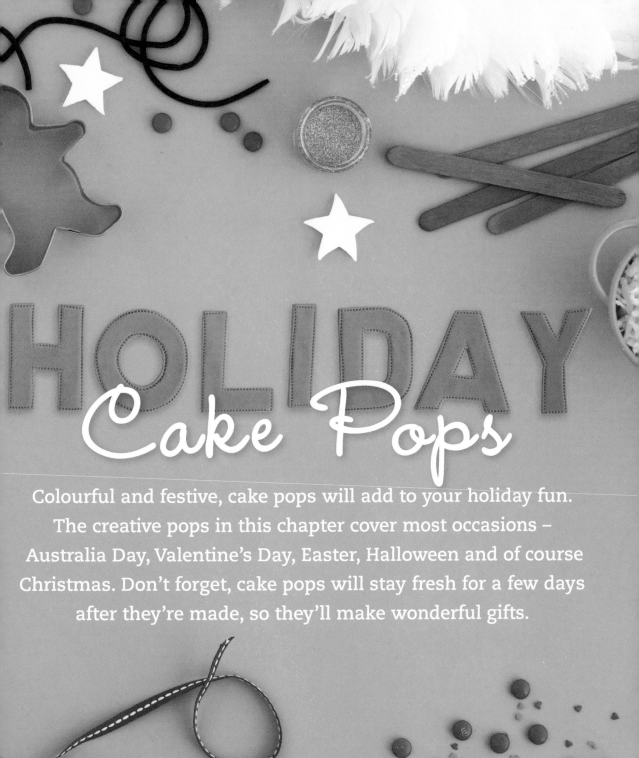

HOLIDAY
Cake Pops

Colourful and festive, cake pops will add to your holiday fun. The creative pops in this chapter cover most occasions – Australia Day, Valentine's Day, Easter, Halloween and of course Christmas. Don't forget, cake pops will stay fresh for a few days after they're made, so they'll make wonderful gifts.

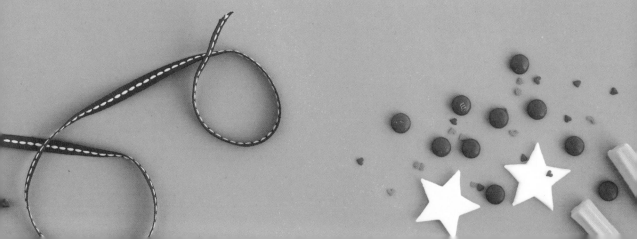

Christmas
PUDDING POPS

180g (5½ ounces)
dark eating
(semi-sweet) chocolate,
chopped coarsely

800g (1½ pounds)
fruit cake

½ cup (125ml) brandy

½ cup (80g) icing
(confectioners') sugar

36 lollipop or paddle
pop sticks

1 quantity royal icing
(see page 9)

36 red candy-coated
chocolates (sixlets)

1 Stir chocolate in a medium heatproof bowl over a medium saucepan of simmering water until smooth (don't let water touch base of bowl).

2 Using hands, crumble cake into a large bowl; stir in chocolate, brandy and sifted icing sugar. Using wet hands, shape level tablespoons of mixture into balls, squeezing firmly. Place balls on a baking paper-lined tray. Freeze 1 hour or refrigerate 3 hours or overnight, until firm.

3 Dip the end of one stick into the royal icing, then push it about halfway into a ball of cake. Return to tray. Repeat with remaining sticks and balls of cake. Place tray in the freezer for about 5 minutes to set.

4 Drizzle royal icing over cake balls, top each with a chocolate; stand pops upright in a styrofoam block (see page 6) until set.

prep + cook time 1 hour (+ freezing & standing)

makes 36

store in an airtight container at a cool room temperature until ready to serve. Cake pops will keep for up to a week.

TIP We used a purchased 800g (1½-pound) fruit cake. Light or dark fruit cake is suitable; use whichever you prefer.

Christmas
ICE-CREAM POPS

2 cups (220g) softened
vanilla ice-cream

1 cup (200g) christmas
pudding, chopped finely

400g (12½-ounce)
block dark eating
(semi-sweet) chocolate

28 wooden
cocktail picks

1 Use fingers to lightly oil two 14-hole ice-cube trays. Line a small oven tray with baking paper.

2 Working quickly, combine ice-cream and pudding in a medium bowl; press mixture into ice-cube tray holes. Freeze about 2 hours or until firm. Release cubes onto the prepared tray; freeze 30 minutes.

3 Meanwhile, to make chocolate curls, slightly warm the chocolate block between your hands; drag the blade of a sharp vegetable peeler evenly down the side to give about ¼ cup chocolate curls (see page 123). Transfer to an airtight container.

4 Chop remaining chocolate. Stir half the chocolate in a medium heatproof bowl over a medium saucepan of simmering water until smooth (don't let water touch base of bowl). Pour into a heatproof jug.

5 Working quickly, insert cocktail picks into ice-cream cubes. Dip half the ice-cream pops, one at a time, into chocolate until covered; return to baking paper-lined tray. Freeze until ready to serve.

6 Repeat melting and dipping with remaining chocolate and ice-cream pops; freeze until ready to serve. Serve pops in paper cases, sprinkled with chocolate curls.

prep + cook time 20 minutes (+ freezing)
makes 28
store in an airtight container in the freezer until ready to serve. Ice-cream pops will keep for up to a week.

TIPS Make the ice-cream pops 1 or 2 days ahead. Use rounded ice-cube trays if possible.

Christmas
WINTER TREES

8 mini waffle cones

3⅓ cups (600g)
madeira cake crumbs

⅓ cup (115g)
strawberry jam

375g (12 ounces)
white chocolate Melts

green food colouring

8 lollipop or paddle
pop sticks

1 tablespoon
silver cachous

8 white icing
star toppers

1 Carefully cut 2.5cm (1 inch) off the wide end of each cone; discard trimmings.

2 Using a fork, combine cake crumbs and jam in a medium bowl. Spoon mixture into cones; press down firmly. Place cones on a baking paper-lined tray. Freeze 1 hour or refrigerate 3 hours or overnight, until set.

3 Stir chocolate in a medium heatproof bowl over a medium saucepan of simmering water until smooth (don't let water touch base of bowl). Tint chocolate green. Pour into a heatproof jug.

4 Dip the end of one stick into the chocolate, then push it about halfway into the base of a cone of cake. Return to tray. Repeat with remaining sticks and cones of cake. Place tray in the freezer for about 5 minutes to set.

5 Spoon chocolate all over a cone to coat; allow excess chocolate to drip back into the jug. Stand upright in a styrofoam block (see page 6) until almost set. Attach cachous and a star, using a little extra melted chocolate, if you need. Repeat with remaining cones, chocolate, cachous and stars. Re-melt chocolate as necessary. Stand upright until set.

prep + cook time 40 minutes (+ freezing & standing)

makes 8

store in an airtight container at a cool room temperature until ready to serve. Cake pops will keep for up to a week.

TIP Icing stars can be purchased at cake decorating suppliers.

Christmas SNOWMEN

1½ cups (240g) firmly packed white chocolate mud cake crumbs

1 tablespoon ready-made vanilla frosting

225g (7 ounces) white chocolate Melts

16 lollipop or paddle pop sticks

⅓ cup (25g) desiccated coconut

8 orange fruit sticks

8 black licorice tubes

60cm (23½-inch) long licorice strap

1 Using a fork, combine cake crumbs and frosting in a medium bowl. Shape tablespoons of mixture into balls, squeezing firmly. Place balls on a baking paper-lined tray. Freeze 1 hour or refrigerate 3 hours or overnight, until firm.

2 Stir chocolate in a medium heatproof bowl over a medium saucepan of simmering water until smooth (don't let water touch base of bowl). Pour into a heatproof jug.

3 Dip the end of one stick into the chocolate, then push it about halfway into a ball of cake. Return to tray. Repeat with remaining sticks and balls of cake. Place tray in the freezer for about 5 minutes to set.

4 Dip one cake pop into the chocolate, rocking back and forth to coat; don't swirl the pop, or it'll break. Allow excess chocolate to drip back into the jug. Sprinkle pop with coconut. Stand cake pop upright in a styrofoam block (see page 6) until set. Repeat with remaining cake pops, chocolate and coconut. Re-melt chocolate as necessary.

5 Cut fruit sticks in half, then cut one end of each into a point for "carrot" noses. Attach noses with a little of the chocolate.

6 Cut licorice tubes in half. Using a 1.5cm (¾-inch) cutter, cut 16 rounds from licorice strap. Secure cut licorice tubes to licorice rounds with a little chocolate to create hats. Cut remaining licorice into small pieces for eyes and mouths. Secure with chocolate. Stand upright until set.

prep + cook time 1 hour (+ freezing & standing)
makes 16
store in an airtight container at a cool room temperature until ready to serve. Cake pops will keep for up to a week.

TIP Use white Candy Melts in place of chocolate Melts for an extra-white finish (see page 7).

Christmas GINGERBREAD MEN

400g (12½ ounces) ginger kisses

375g (12 ounces) white chocolate Melts

brown and orange food colouring

8 paddle pop sticks

1 quantity royal icing (see page 9)

24 red mini M&M's

1 Crumble kisses (with filling) into a medium bowl. Using hands, knead the mixture into a ball. Roll the mixture flat between sheets of baking paper to a 1.5cm (¾-inch) thickness. Transfer, on baking paper, to a tray; refrigerate 20 minutes.

2 Using a 9cm (3¾-inch) cutter, cut out as many gingerbread men as possible. Re-roll mixture to cut out a total of eight men. Place on baking paper-lined trays; freeze 1 hour or refrigerate 3 hours or overnight, until firm.

3 Stir chocolate in a medium heatproof bowl over a medium saucepan of simmering water until smooth (don't let water touch base of bowl). Tint light brown using brown and orange colouring. Pour into a heatproof jug.

4 Dip 4.5cm (1¾ inches) of the end of one paddle pop stick into chocolate; place coated end of paddle pop stick over back of gingerbread man, pressing lightly until beginning to set. Return to tray. Repeat with remaining sticks and gingerbread men. Place in freezer for about 5 minutes to set.

5 Re-melt chocolate if necessary. Working quickly, hold a gingerbread man over the jug of chocolate; spoon chocolate over man to cover. Allow excess chocolate to drip back into the jug. Stand cake pop upright in a styrofoam block (see page 6) until set. Repeat with remaining men and chocolate.

6 Spoon royal icing into a piping bag fitted with 4mm (¼-inch) tube. Pipe around outline of men. Pipe face and secure three M&M's to each gingerbread man for buttons. Stand upright at room temperature until set.

prep + cook time 1 hour 10 minutes (+ freezing & standing)
makes 8
note Ginger kisses are small cream-filled sponge cakes, about 25g (¾ ounce) each.
store in an airtight container at a cool room temperature until ready to serve. Cake pops will keep for up to a week.

Easter
EGG POPS

4 cups (640g) firmly packed chocolate cake crumbs

⅓ cup (100g) ready-made milk chocolate frosting

375g (12 ounces) white Candy Melts (see page 7)

purple, yellow, green and blue food colouring

18 lollipop or paddle pop sticks

1 tablespoon each purple, yellow, green, and blue sanding sugar

1 Using a fork, combine cake crumbs and frosting in a medium bowl. Shape level tablespoons of the mixture into ovals, squeezing firmly. Place ovals on a baking paper-lined tray; freeze 1 hour, or refrigerate 3 hours or overnight, until firm.
2 Stir Candy Melts in a medium heatproof bowl over a medium saucepan of simmering water until smooth (don't let water touch base of bowl). Divide Melts evenly between four small bowls; tint pale purple, yellow, green and blue.
3 Dip the end of one stick into the Melts, then push the stick about halfway into an oval of cake. Return to tray. Repeat with remaining sticks and ovals of cake, alternating Melt colours. Place in the freezer for about 5 minutes to set.
4 Dip one cake pop into the purple Melts, rocking back and forth to coat; don't swirl the pop, or it'll break. Allow excess to drip back into the bowl. Stand cake pop upright in a styrofoam block (see page 6) until set. Repeat with remaining cake pops, alternating the Melt colours. Re-melt Candy Melts as necessary.
5 Working with one colour at a time, spoon remaining Melts into small piping bags. Pipe dots onto cake pops, then press the corresponding coloured sugar onto the dots. We used blue sugar on purple eggs, yellow sugar on blue eggs, green sugar on yellow eggs and purple sugar on green eggs. Stand upright until set. Don't refrigerate or the sugar will dissolve.
prep + cook time 50 minutes (+ freezing & standing)
makes 18
tip If you can't find Candy Melts, use white chocolate Melts.
store in an airtight container at a cool room temperature until ready to serve. Cake pops will keep for up to a week.

New Year's Eve
GLITTER BALLS

4 cups (680g) firmly packed butter cake crumbs

⅓ cup (100g) ready-made vanilla frosting

275g (9 ounces) white chocolate Melts

38 lollipop or paddle pop sticks

5g (¼ ounce) hologram silver edible glitter

1 Using a fork, combine cake crumbs and frosting in a medium bowl. Shape three level teaspoons of mixture at a time into balls, squeezing firmly. Place balls on a baking paper-lined tray; freeze 1 hour or refrigerate 3 hours or overnight, until firm.

2 Stir chocolate in a medium heatproof bowl over a medium saucepan of simmering water until smooth (don't let water touch base of bowl). Pour into a heatproof jug.

3 Dip the end of one stick into the chocolate, then push it about halfway into a ball of cake. Return to tray. Repeat with remaining sticks and balls of cake. Place tray in the freezer for about 5 minutes to set.

4 Dip one cake pop into the chocolate, rocking back and forth to coat; don't swirl the pop, or it'll break. Allow excess chocolate to drip back into the jug. Sprinkle the pop with glitter. Stand upright in a styrofoam block (see page 6) until set. Repeat with remaining cake pops. Re-melt chocolate as necessary.

prep + cook time 1 hour (+ freezing & standing)
makes 38
store in an airtight container at a cool room temperature until ready to serve. Cake pops will keep for up to a week.

TIP Use white Candy Melts in place of chocolate Melts for a whiter finish (see page 7).

Valentine's Day
LOVE HEARTS

4 cups (640g) firmly packed chocolate cake crumbs

⅓ cup (100g) ready-made chocolate frosting

275g (9 ounces) white chocolate Melts

red food colouring

28 lollipop or paddle pop sticks

1 tablespoon each pink and red heart-shaped sprinkles

14 sugar hearts

1 Grease and line a deep 15cm (6-inch) square cake pan with baking paper. Combine cake crumbs and frosting in a medium bowl. Press mixture evenly into the pan; cover; freeze 1 hour or refrigerate 3 hours or overnight, until firm.

2 Using a 4.5cm (1¾-inch) heart-shaped cutter, cut 28 hearts from the cake mixture. Place on a baking paper-lined tray, freeze 1 hour, or refrigerate 3 hours or overnight, until firm.

3 Stir chocolate in a medium heatproof bowl over a medium saucepan of simmering water until smooth (don't let water touch base of bowl); tint red. Pour into a heatproof jug.

4 Dip the end of one stick into chocolate, then push the stick about halfway into a cake heart. Repeat with remaining sticks and hearts. Return to tray. Place in freezer for about 5 minutes to set.

5 Dip one cake pop into the chocolate, rocking back and forth to coat; don't swirl the pop, or it'll break. Allow excess chocolate to drip back into the jug. Scatter pop with combined sprinkles. Stand upright in a styrofoam block (see page 6) until set. Repeat with remaining cake pops, decorating another 13 with sprinkles, and attaching sugar hearts to the other 14 with a little of the melted chocolate. Stand upright until set.

prep + cook time 55 minutes (+ freezing & standing)

makes 28

store in an airtight container at a cool room temperature until ready to serve. Cake pops will keep for up to a week.

TIP Use red Candy Melts in place of tinted chocolate Melts if you like (see page 7).

Australia Day LAMINGTON POPS

4½ cups (540g) firmly packed sponge cake crumbs

½ cup (150g) ready-made vanilla frosting

375g (12 ounces) dark chocolate Melts

32 lollipop or paddle pop sticks

1½ cups (120g) desiccated coconut

1 Using a fork, combine cake crumbs and frosting in a medium bowl. Using wet hands, shape level tablespoons of the mixture into balls, squeezing firmly. Place balls on a baking paper-lined tray. Freeze 1 hour, or refrigerate 3 hours or overnight.

2 Melt chocolate in a medium heatproof bowl over a medium saucepan of simmering water until smooth (don't let water touch base of bowl). Transfer to a heatproof jug.

3 Dip the end of one stick into the chocolate, then push it about halfway into a ball of cake. Return to tray. Repeat with remaining sticks and balls of cake. Place tray in the freezer for about 5 minutes to set.

4 Place coconut in a shallow dish.

5 Dip one cake pop into the chocolate, rocking back and forth to coat; don't swirl the pop, or it'll break. Allow excess chocolate to drip back into the jug. Stand cake pop upright in a styrofoam block (see page 6). Before chocolate sets, sprinkle and press on coconut to cover the pop. Repeat with remaining cake pops. Re-melt chocolate as necessary. Stand upright until set.

prep + cook time 1 hour 10 minutes (+ freezing & standing)

makes 32

store cake pops in an airtight container at a cool room temperature until ready to serve. They will keep for up to a week.

Halloween
LITTLE DEVILS

2 cups (320g) firmly packed chocolate mud cake crumbs

1 tablespoon ready-made chocolate frosting

375g (12 ounces) white chocolate Melts

red food colouring

14 lollipop or paddle pop sticks

28 dark (semi-sweet) Choc Bits

7 red mini M&M's, halved

¼ quantity royal icing

black food colouring

1 Using a fork, combine cake crumbs and frosting in a medium bowl. Shape level tablespoons of the mixture into balls, squeezing firmly. Place balls on a baking paper-lined tray; freeze 1 hour or refrigerate 3 hours or overnight, until firm.

2 Stir white chocolate in a medium heatproof bowl over a medium saucepan of simmering water until smooth (don't let water touch base of bowl); tint chocolate red. Pour into a heatproof jug.

3 Dip the end of one stick into the chocolate, then push it about halfway into a ball of cake. Return to tray. Repeat with remaining sticks and balls of cake. Place in the freezer for about 5 minutes to set.

4 Stand cake pops upright in a styrofoam block (see page 6). Attach 2 Choc Bits to each pop with a little of the melted chocolate, to make horns. Stand upright until set.

5 Re-melt red chocolate as necessary. Dip one cake pop into the chocolate, rocking back and forth to coat; don't swirl the pop, or it'll break. Allow excess chocolate to drip back into the jug. Stand upright in styrofoam. Before chocolate completely sets, attach an M&M-half for a nose. Repeat with remaining cake pops, chocolate and M&M's.

6 Tint royal icing black. Spoon icing into a small piping bag fitted with a 3mm (⅛-inch) tube. Pipe eyebrows, eyes and grin onto pops. Stand upright until set.

prep + cook time 50 minutes (+ freezing & standing)
makes 14

store in an airtight container at a cool room temperature until ready to serve. Cake pops will keep for up to a week. Pipe eyebrows, eyes and grin on the day of serving.

TIP Use red Candy Melts in place of tinted chocolate Melts, if you like (see page 7).

Halloween
BLACK SPIDERS

2½ cups (400g) firmly packed chocolate mud cake crumbs

½ cup (150g) ready-made milk chocolate frosting

375g (12 ounces) dark chocolate Melts

22 lollipop or paddle pop sticks

4.5 metres (4½ yards) licorice bootlaces

44 mini M&M's

1 Using a fork, combine cake crumbs and frosting in a medium bowl. Using wet hands, shape level tablespoons of the mixture into balls, squeezing firmly. Place balls on a baking paper-lined tray.

2 Stir chocolate in a medium heatproof bowl over a medium saucepan of simmering water until smooth (don't let water touch base of bowl). Pour into a heatproof jug.

3 Dip the end of one stick into the chocolate, then push it about halfway into a ball of cake. Return to tray. Repeat with remaining sticks and balls of cake. Place in the freezer for about 5 minutes to set.

4 Cut licorice into 2.5cm (1-inch) lengths.

5 Decorate about four cake pops at a time. Dip a cake pop into the chocolate, rocking back and forth to coat; don't swirl the pop, or it'll break. Allow excess chocolate to drip back into the jug. Stand pop upright in a styrofoam block (see page 6) about 30 seconds or until firm enough to hold licorice in place. Insert eight licorice pieces into sides of pop for legs. Decorate with M&M's for eyes. Stand upright until set. Repeat with remaining cake pops. Re-melt chocolate as necessary.

prep + cook time 1 hour (+ freezing & standing)

makes 22

store in an airtight container at a cool room temperature until ready to serve. Cake pops will keep for up to a week. Don't refrigerate, as colouring on M&M's will run.

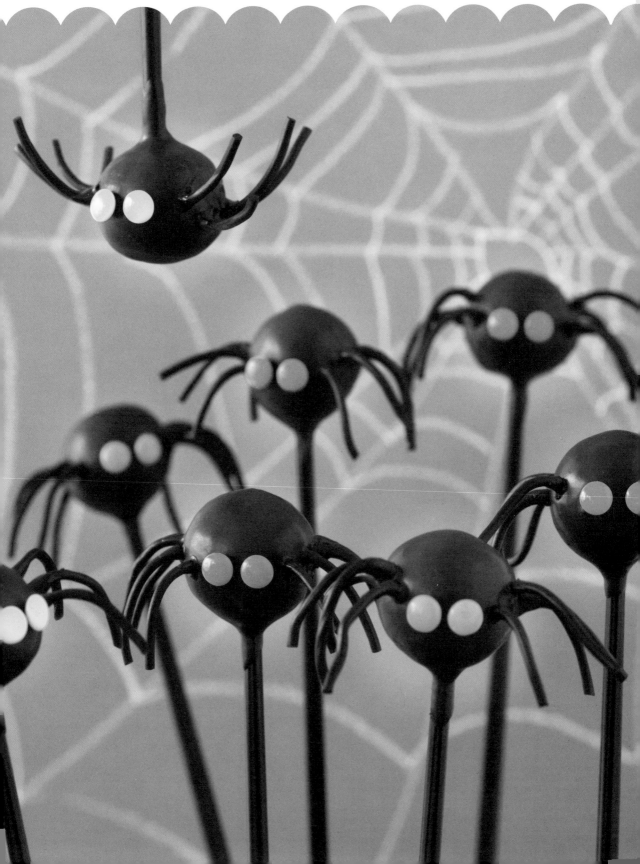

BIRTHDAY
Cake Pops

Don't be fooled, this chapter isn't just for kids. It's packed with cake pops for everyone to enjoy. Sticky date toffee pops, chilli chocolate pops and tiramisu cups – there's something here to suit every birthday party.

Chocolate
CHERRY POPS

¼ cup (60ml) thickened (heavy) cream

3 x 52g (1½-ounce) cherry ripe chocolate bars, chopped coarsely

2½ cups (400g) firmly packed chocolate mud cake crumbs

375g (12 ounces) white chocolate Melts

red food colouring

24 lollipop or paddle pop sticks

6 green sour worms

1 Bring cream to the boil in a small saucepan; remove from heat. Add cherry ripe, stand 1 minute; stir until combined.

2 Combine cake crumbs and cherry ripe mixture in a medium bowl. Using wet hands, shape level tablespoons of the mixture into balls, squeezing firmly. Place balls on a baking paper-lined tray; freeze 1 hour or refrigerate 3 hours or overnight, until firm.

3 Stir white chocolate in a medium heatproof bowl over a medium saucepan of simmering water until smooth (don't let water touch base of bowl); tint chocolate red. Transfer to a heatproof jug.

4 Dip the end of one stick into the chocolate, then push it about halfway into a ball of cake. Return to tray. Repeat with remaining sticks and balls of cake. Place tray in the freezer for about 5 minutes to set.

5 Cut sour worms into quarters lengthways, to make stems.

6 Dip one cake pop into the chocolate, rocking back and forth to coat; don't swirl the pop, or it'll break. Allow excess chocolate to drip back into the jug. Stand pop upright in a styrofoam block (see page 6). Before chocolate completely sets, attach a piece of sour worm to the top of the cherry. Repeat with remaining cake pops, chocolate and sour worm pieces. Re-melt chocolate as necessary.

prep + cook time 1 hour (+ freezing & standing)
makes 24
store in an airtight container at a cool room temperature until ready to serve. Cake pops will keep for up to a week.

TIP Use red Candy Melts in place of tinted chocolate Melts if you like (see page 7).

Buttery salted
POPCORN CAKES

50g (1½ ounces) cream cheese, softened

20g (¾ ounce) butter, softened

¾ cup (120g) icing (confectioners') sugar

4½ cups (540g) firmly packed sponge cake crumbs

375g (12 ounces) white chocolate Melts

32 lollipop or paddle pop sticks

3¼ cups (35g) popped buttered, salted popcorn, chopped coarsely

1 Beat cream cheese and butter in a small bowl with an electric mixer until light and fluffy; gradually beat in sifted icing sugar.

2 Stir cream cheese mixture into cake crumbs in a medium bowl. Using wet hands, shape level tablespoons of the mixture into balls, squeezing firmly. Place balls on a baking paper-lined tray. Freeze 1 hour, or refrigerate 3 hours or overnight, until firm.

3 Melt chocolate in a medium heatproof bowl over a medium saucepan of simmering water (don't let water touch base of bowl). Transfer to a heatproof jug.

4 Dip the end of one stick into the chocolate, then push it about halfway into a ball of cake. Return to tray. Repeat with remaining sticks and balls of cake. Place in the freezer for about 5 minutes to set.

5 Dip one cake pop into the chocolate, rocking back and forth to coat; don't swirl the pop, or it'll break. Allow excess chocolate to drip back into the jug. Stand pop upright in a styrofoam block (see page 6) until firm enough to hold popcorn in place. Press popcorn pieces all over cake pop. Repeat with remaining cake pops, chocolate and popcorn. Re-melt chocolate as necessary. Stand upright until set.

prep + cook time 1 hour (+ freezing & standing)

makes 32

store in an airtight container at a cool room temperature until ready to serve. Cake pops can be made a day ahead.

Cookies & cream
CAKE POPS

300g (9½ ounces)
cream-filled
chocolate biscuits

1 cup (300g) ready-
made vanilla frosting

360g (11½ ounces)
cookies & cream
chocolate,
chopped coarsely

24 lollipop sticks or
bamboo skewers

180g (5½ ounces) dark
chocolate Melts

½ cup (85g) ebony &
ivory sprinkles

24 coloured
drinking straws

1 Process biscuits in a food processor until mixture resembles fine crumbs. Using a fork, combine biscuit crumbs and frosting in a medium bowl. Roll level tablespoons of the mixture into balls. Place balls on a baking paper-lined tray, freeze 1 hour or refrigerate 3 hours or overnight, until firm.

2 Stir cookies and cream chocolate in a medium heatproof bowl over a medium saucepan of simmering water until smooth (don't let water touch base of bowl). Transfer to a heatproof jug.

3 Dip the end of one stick into the chocolate, then push it about halfway into a cookie ball. Return to tray. Repeat with remaining sticks and cookie balls. Place in the freezer for about 5 minutes to set.

4 Dip one cake pop into the chocolate, rocking back and forth to coat; don't swirl the pop, or it'll break. Allow excess chocolate to drip back into the jug. Stand pop upright in a styrofoam block (see page 6) until set. Repeat with remaining cake pops. Re-melt chocolate as necessary.

5 Stir dark chocolate in a small heatproof bowl over a small saucepan of simmering water until smooth (don't let water touch base of bowl). Dip half of each cake pop into dark chocolate and scatter with sprinkles. Slide a straw over each stick, pushing up into the chocolate. Stand upright to set.

prep + cook time 35 minutes (+ freezing & standing)
makes 24

store in an airtight container at a cool room temperature until ready to serve. Cake pops will keep for up to a week.

Index

Rocky road
CAKE POPS

300g (9½ ounces) chocolate brownies

1 cup (170g) firmly packed butter cake crumbs

⅓ cup (100g) ready-made chocolate frosting

¼ cup (15g) mini mallows, halved

¼ cup (50g) red glacé cherries, chopped coarsely

¼ cup (35g) roasted unsalted peanuts, chopped coarsely

100g (3 ounces) dark (semi-sweet) eating chocolate, chopped coarsely

24 lollipop or paddle pop sticks

½ cup (40g) flaked almonds

1 Break brownies into small crumbs in a medium bowl. Using a fork, combine brownie crumbs, cake crumbs and frosting.

2 Stir in mini mallows, cherries and peanuts until combined. Roll level tablespoons of the mixture into balls. Place balls on a baking paper-lined tray, freeze 1 hour or refrigerate 3 hours or overnight, until firm.

3 Stir chocolate in a small heatproof bowl over a small saucepan of simmering water until smooth (don't let water touch base of bowl). Pour into a heatproof jug.

4 Dip the end of one stick into the chocolate, then push it about halfway into a ball of cake. Return to tray. Repeat with remaining sticks and balls of cake. Place in the freezer for about 5 minutes to set.

5 Meanwhile, toast almonds, by stirring them over medium heat in a medium frying pan, until golden brown. Transfer to small heatproof bowl; cool.

6 Re-melt the chocolate if necessary. Dip the top half of each cake pop into melted chocolate, then into toasted almonds. Stand pops upright in a styrofoam block (see page 6) until set.

prep + cook time 40 minutes (+ freezing & standing)

makes 24

tips Ready-made brownies can be found in the bakery section of most supermarkets. If you can't find mini mallows, finely chop regular marshmallows with lightly oiled scissors. For a child's party, dip the pops in coloured sprinkles instead of almonds.

store in an airtight container at a cool room temperature until ready to serve. Cake pops will keep for up to a week.

Strawberry
CHEESECAKE POPS

360g (11½ ounces) frozen strawberry cheesecake, thawed

2½ cups (425g) firmly packed butter cake crumbs

375g (12 ounces) white chocolate Melts

red food colouring

18 lollipop or paddle pop sticks

18 green drinking straws

⅓ cup (70g) green sprinkles

50g (1½ ounces) ready-made white icing

green food colouring

cornflour (cornstarch)

1 Using a fork, combine cheesecake, including biscuit base, and cake crumbs in a medium bowl. Roll level tablespoons of the mixture into strawberry shapes. Place on a baking paper-lined tray, freeze 1 hour or refrigerate 3 hours or overnight, until firm.

2 Stir chocolate in a medium heatproof bowl over a medium saucepan of simmering water until smooth (don't let water touch base of bowl). Tint chocolate red. Pour into a heatproof jug.

3 Dip the end of one stick into the chocolate, then push it about halfway into a strawberry shape. Return to tray. Repeat with remaining sticks and strawberries. Place in the freezer for about 5 minutes to set.

4 Dip one cake pop into the chocolate, rocking back and forth to coat; don't swirl the pop, or it'll break. Allow excess chocolate to drip back into the jug. Slide a straw over the stick, pushing up into the chocolate. Stand pop upright in a styrofoam block (see page 6); scatter with sprinkles. Repeat with remaining cake pops, chocolate, straws and sprinkles. Re-melt chocolate as necessary.

5 Tint icing green, knead on a surface lightly dusted with cornflour until it loses its stickiness. Roll onto a lightly dusted surface until icing is 3mm (⅛ inch) thick. Using a 2.5cm (1-inch) star cutter, cut 18 stars from rolled out icing. Working quickly, use a frilling tool to frill edges of stars, making them look like calyxes. Thread frilled leaves onto sticks, securing with a little chocolate. Stand until set.

prep + cook time 45 minutes (+ freezing & standing)
makes 18 **store** cake pops without green calyxes in the refrigerator until ready to serve. They will keep for up to 2 days.

White chocolate
PASSIONFRUIT POPS

1 white chocolate
mud cake (see page 10)

100g (3 ounces)
white eating
chocolate, chopped

¼ cup (60ml)
passionfruit pulp

375g (12 ounces)
white chocolate Melts

-----

23 lollipop or paddle
pop sticks

-----

passionfruit icing

-----

2 tablespoons
passionfruit pulp

½ cup (80g) icing
(confectioners') sugar

-----

1 Using your hands, crumble two-thirds of the cake into a large bowl. Reserve remaining cake for another use.

2 Stir chopped chocolate in a small heatproof bowl over a small saucepan of simmering water until smooth (don't let water touch base of bowl).

3 Stir passionfruit pulp and melted chocolate into cake crumbs. Shape rounded tablespoons of mixture into balls, squeezing firmly; place on a baking paper-lined tray. Cover; freeze 1 hour or refrigerate 3 hours or overnight, until firm.

4 Stir chocolate Melts in a medium heatproof bowl over a medium saucepan of simmering water until smooth (don't let water touch base of bowl). Pour into a heatproof jug.

5 Dip the end of one stick into the chocolate, then push it about halfway into a ball of cake. Return to tray. Repeat with remaining sticks and balls of cake; freeze for about 5 minutes to set.

6 Dip one cake pop into the chocolate, rocking back and forth to coat; don't swirl the pop, or it'll break. Allow excess chocolate to drip back into the jug. Stand pop upright in a styrofoam block (see page 6) until set. Repeat with remaining cake pops. Re-melt chocolate as necessary.

7 Meanwhile, make passionfruit icing.

8 Spoon icing into a piping bag fitted with a 3mm (⅛-inch) plain tube. Pipe icing over cake pops. Stand until set.

passionfruit icing Strain passionfruit pulp through a fine sieve into a small bowl; discard seeds. Add sifted icing sugar; mix well.

prep + cook time 1 hour 40 minutes (+ freezing & standing)
makes 23 **tip** Use white Candy Melts in place of chocolate Melts for an extra-white finish (see page 7).

store in an airtight container at a cool room temperature until ready to serve. Cake pops will keep for up to a week.

Pretty pink
BUTTERFLIES

3⅓ cups (600g) firmly packed madeira cake crumbs

⅓ cup (110g) raspberry jam

375g (12 ounces) white chocolate Melts

rose pink food colouring

25 lollipop or paddle pop sticks

1 tablespoon pink sprinkles

1 Using a fork, combine cake crumbs and jam in a medium bowl. Shape level tablespoons of mixture into balls, squeezing firmly. Place balls on a baking paper-lined tray; freeze 1 hour or refrigerate 3 hours or overnight, until firm.

2 Stir chocolate in a medium heatproof bowl over a medium saucepan of simmering water until smooth (don't let water touch base of bowl). Transfer one-quarter of the chocolate to a small bowl; tint rose pink.

3 Dip the end of one stick into the white chocolate, then push it about halfway into a ball of cake. Return to tray. Repeat with remaining sticks and balls of cake. Place in the freezer for about 5 minutes to set.

4 Dip one cake pop into the chocolate, rocking back and forth to coat; don't swirl the pop, or it'll break. Allow excess chocolate to drip back into the jug. Stand pop upright in a styrofoam block (see page 6). Scatter cake pops with sprinkles before chocolate sets. Stand upright until set.

5 Re-melt pink chocolate if necessary. Spoon into a piping bag, snip a small hole from one corner of piping bag. Using picture as a guide, pipe 50 x 6cm (2½-inch) single butterfly wings onto sheets of baking paper (see page 121); stand until chocolate sets. Pipe a small line of chocolate onto one wing; join second wing and hold about one minute or until chocolate is set. Repeat with remaining wings and chocolate.

6 Carefully attach butterflies to top of cake pops with a little melted chocolate. Stand upright until set.

prep + cook time 1 hour 30 minutes (+ freezing & standing)
makes 25

TIPS See page 121 for more information on piping chocolate. Use white Candy Melts in place of chocolate Melts for an extra-white finish (see page 7). Store cake pops in an airtight container at a cool room temperature until ready to serve. They will keep for up to a week.

Cute little
CUPCAKE POPS

350g (11-ounce) banana cake with frosting

375g (12 ounces) white chocolate Melts

sky blue, rose pink and lemon yellow food colouring

12 lollipop or paddle pop sticks

400g (12½ ounces) ready-made white icing

cornflour (cornstarch)

1 tablespoon coloured sprinkles

1 tablespoon hundreds and thousands

12 red Smarties

1 Process cake and frosting until mixture just comes together. Push tablespoons of the mixture firmly into a 12-hole (1-tablespoon/20ml) mini muffin pan. Place pan in the freezer, freeze 1 hour.

2 Carefully remove cakes from pan using a flat-bladed knife. Reshape cakes, if necessary.

3 Stir chocolate in a medium heatproof bowl over a medium saucepan of simmering water until smooth (don't let water touch base of bowl). Divide chocolate evenly between three small bowls; tint pale blue, pink and yellow.

4 Dip the end of one stick into the chocolate, then push it about halfway into the base of a cake. Return to tray. Repeat with remaining sticks and cakes, alternating chocolate colours. Place in the freezer for about 5 minutes to set.

5 Dip one cake pop into the chocolate, rocking back and forth to coat; don't swirl the pop, or it'll break. Allow excess chocolate to drip back into the jug. Stand pop upright in a styrofoam block (see page 6) until set. Repeat with remaining cake pops and chocolate, alternating colours (you will have four pops in each colour). Re-melt chocolate as necessary.

6 Divide icing into three balls. Tint icing pale blue, pink and yellow. Wrap each ball in plastic. Dust a surface lightly with cornflour. Unwrap blue icing and roll into a 5mm (2-inch) sausage. Cut into four equal lengths. Brush the top of four cake pops with a little water. Wrap icing in a spiral on top of pops. Repeat with remaining icings.

7 Lightly brush icing with a little water, scatter with sprinkles and hundreds and thousands. Re-melt chocolate if necessary. Use a little chocolate to secure Smarties to tops of cakes.

prep + cook time 1½ hours (+ freezing & standing)
makes 12

TIPS Store cake pops in an airtight container at a cool room temperature until ready to serve. They will keep for up to a week. Don't refrigerate, as colouring on Smarties will run.

Sticky date
TOFFEE POPS

100g (3 ounces)
butter, chopped

½ cup (110g)
firmly packed light
brown sugar

¼ cup (60ml) thickened
(heavy) cream

24 (480g) fresh dates

2 cups (340g)
firmly packed butter
cake crumbs

24 lollipop or paddle
pop sticks

2 cups (440g)
white sugar

½ cup (125ml) water

1 Melt butter in a small saucepan; add brown sugar, stir to dissolve. Bring mixture to the boil; add cream, cook, stirring, about 2 minutes or until mixture is smooth and golden brown. Transfer mixture to a large heatproof bowl; refrigerate 2 hours or until just firm.

2 Meanwhile, using a small knife, cut a slit in the top of each date. Using the tip of the knife, remove seeds without piercing the skin of the dates.

3 Add cake crumbs to the large bowl with cold caramel mixture. Using hands, mix well. Fill a piping bag, fitted with a 1.5cm (¾-inch) tube, with cake mixture. Pipe small amounts of cake mixture into dates. Push sticks into open end of dates, pushing halfway up the length of each date. Lightly press each filled date between hands to flatten slightly. Place dates on a baking paper-lined tray; freeze for 30 minutes.

4 Combine half the white sugar and half the water in a small saucepan; stir over a medium heat until sugar is dissolved. Bring to the boil; boil, uncovered, without stirring, about 10 minutes or until mixture turns a toffee colour. Remove from heat, allow bubbles to subside. Remove half of the dates from the freezer. Working quickly dip one date at a time into toffee to coat completely. Stand toffee-dipped dates upright in a styrofoam block (see page 6) until set. Repeat with remaining sugar, water and dates.

prep + cook time 50 minutes (+ refrigeration & standing)
makes 24
tips Once they are toffee-coated, don't refrigerate the pops, as the toffee will dissolve. Serve pops within 2 hours of making.

Chilli chocolate
TRUFFLE POPS

2 fresh long red chillies

500g (1 pound)
dark (semi-sweet)
chocolate Melts

⅓ cup (80ml) thickened
(heavy) cream

½ cup (110g)
white sugar

¼ cup (60ml) water

red food colouring

12 cocktail forks

1 sheet gold leaf

1 Preheat oven to 150°C/300°F. Finely chop one of the chillies.
2 Stir 1⅓ cups (200g) of the chocolate and cream in a small saucepan over low heat until smooth; stir in the chopped chilli. Transfer mixture to a small bowl; refrigerate 3 hours.
3 Meanwhile, thinly slice remaining chilli. Place on a baking paper-lined oven tray; cook about 10 minutes or until chilli is dehydrated but still has its colour. Cool on tray. Combine sugar and the water in a small saucepan, stir over medium heat until sugar is dissolved. Bring to the boil; boil, uncovered, without stirring, about 10 minutes or until mixture turns a toffee colour. Remove from heat, allow bubbles to subside; tint red. Pour toffee mixture over chilli on tray. Cool.
4 Working with one-quarter of the chilli-chocolate mixture at a time (keep remaining mixture in the refrigerator), roll heaped teaspoons of the mixture into balls. Place on a baking paper-lined tray. Refrigerate truffles about 1 hour or until firm.
5 Stir remaining chocolate in a medium heatproof bowl over a medium saucepan of simmering water (don't let water touch base of bowl). Dip the end of one cocktail fork into chocolate, then push it halfway into a truffle. Return to tray. Repeat with remaining forks and truffles. Refrigerate 30 minutes.
6 Dip one truffle pop into the chocolate, rocking back and forth to coat; don't swirl the pop, or it'll break. Allow excess chocolate to drip back into the jug. Stand pop upright in a styrofoam block (see page 6) until almost set. Repeat with remaining truffle pops. Re-melt chocolate as necessary.
7 Break chilli toffee into small shards; push two or three pieces of toffee into the bottom of each truffle, just as chocolate coating begins to set. Using small tweezers, decorate truffle pops with pieces of gold leaf, taking care not to touch leaf with hands. Serve within 2 hours of making.
prep + cook time 1 hour 10 minutes (+ refrigeration & standing)
makes 12

Tiny chocolate
TIRAMISU CUPS

200g (6½ ounces) dark (semi-sweet) chocolate Melts

20 foil petit four cases

20 bamboo skewers

⅓ cup (125g) mascarpone cheese

⅓ cup (80ml) coffee liqueur

100g (3 ounces) sponge cake

20 dark (semi-sweet) chocolate-coated coffee beans

2 tablespoons cocoa powder

1 Stir chocolate in a small heatproof bowl over a small saucepan of simmering water until smooth (don't let water touch base of bowl). Using a paintbrush, paint melted chocolate thickly on inside of the foil cases. Place on a tray. Refrigerate 30 minutes or until set. Reserve leftover chocolate.
2 Gently peel away foil cases from chocolate. Place chocolate cups flat on a bench. Using the pointed end of a skewer, gently push a hole, using a twisting motion, through the centre of the base of each chocolate cup. Re-melt chocolate; paint a second coat, avoiding the holes. Return to tray, refrigerate until set. Reserve remaining chocolate.
3 Re-melt reserved chocolate. Remove chocolate cups from the refrigerator; turn upside-down on a baking paper-lined tray. Dip the end of one skewer into the chocolate, then gently push it through the hole of a cup, ensuring the skewer remains straight. Repeat with remaining skewers and cups. Transfer to refrigerator; allow to set completely.
4 Stir mascarpone and 1 tablespoon of the liqueur in a small bowl until combined. Pour remaining liqueur into a small shallow bowl. Cut cake into 1cm (½-inch) cubes. Dip cubes of cake into liqueur, one at a time, then thread onto the skewer inside each chocolate cup. Stand pops upright in a styrofoam block (see page 6). Top each cup with a small dollop of the mascarpone mixture and a coffee bean. Just before serving, dust with sifted cocoa.
prep + cook time 1 hour (+ refrigeration)
makes 20

TIPS Store tiramisu
cups upright in the
refrigerator until ready to
serve. They are best made
on the day of serving.

Chocolate cookie
CAPPUCCINO POPS

300g (9½ ounces)
cream-filled
chocolate biscuits,
chopped coarsely

1 cup (300g)
ready-made rich
chocolate fudge frosting

375g (12 ounces)
white chocolate Melts

25 bamboo skewers

25 large coffee-flavoured
chocolate buttons

68g (2 ounces)
peppermint Life Savers

½ cup (50g) hot
chocolate flakes

1 Process biscuits until fine. Using a fork, combine crumbs and frosting in a medium bowl. Shape level tablespoons of the mixture into balls, squeezing firmly. Place on a baking paper-lined tray; freeze 1 hour or refrigerate 3 hours or overnight, until firm.

2 Stir white chocolate in a medium heatproof bowl over a medium saucepan of simmering water until smooth (don't let water touch base of bowl). Pour into a heatproof jug.

3 Dip the end of one skewer into the chocolate, then push it about halfway into a ball of cake. Return to tray. Repeat with remaining skewers and balls of cake. Place in the freezer for 5 minutes to set.

4 To make saucers, place chocolate buttons flat on a board. Using the pointed end of a skewer, gently push a hole, using a twisting motion, through the centre of each button.

5 Using a sharp knife, cut the top-third off balls to create a flat top; discard off-cuts. Dip one cake pop into the chocolate, rocking back and forth to coat; don't swirl the pop, or it'll break. Allow excess chocolate to drip back into the jug. Stand pop upright in a styrofoam block (see page 6). When chocolate is almost set, thread a button onto each stick, pushing up to the base of the cake pop. Repeat with remaining pops. Re-melt chocolate as necessary.

6 Cut Life Savers in half; push into the side of each cake pop to form handles. Sprinkle chocolate flakes over tops of pops.

prep + cook time 1 hour (+ freezing & standing)
makes 25 **store** cake pops in an airtight container at a cool room temperature until ready to serve. They will keep for up to a week. Top with flakes just before serving.

birthday cake pops

TIP Hot chocolate flakes are usually sold in the coffee section of the supermarket.

Chocolate caramel
MUD POPS

1 x caramel mud cake
(see page 11)

180g (5½ ounces)
white eating chocolate,
chopped

375g (12 ounces) milk
chocolate Melts

25 cocktail toothpicks

¼ cup (50g) chocolate
sprinkles

1 Using your hands, crumble two-thirds of the cake into a large bowl. Reserve remaining cake for another use.
2 Stir white chocolate in a medium heatproof bowl over a medium saucepan of simmering water until smooth (don't let water touch base of bowl).
3 Stir melted chocolate into cake crumbs. Using wet hands, shape rounded tablespoons of the mixture into balls, squeezing firmly. Place on a baking paper-lined tray. Freeze 1 hour or refrigerate 3 hours or overnight, until firm.
4 Stir milk chocolate in a medium heatproof bowl over a medium saucepan of simmering water until smooth (don't let water touch base of bowl). Pour into a heatproof jug.
5 Dip the end of one toothpick into the chocolate, then push it about halfway into a ball of cake. Return to tray. Repeat with remaining toothpicks and balls of cake. Place tray in the freezer for about 5 minutes to set.
6 Dip one cake pop into the chocolate, rocking back and forth to coat; don't swirl the pop, or it'll break. Allow excess chocolate to drip back into the jug; scatter with sprinkles. Stand pop upright on a sheet of baking paper until set. Repeat with remaining cake pops, chocolate and sprinkles. Re-melt chocolate as necessary.

prep + cook time 40 minutes (+ freezing & standing)
makes 25
store in an airtight container at a cool room temperature until ready to serve. Cake pops will keep for up to a week.

birthday cake pops

Gift wrapping

There's a variety of pretty paper patty cases available these days. Turn the pops upside-down and place them in the cases on a cake stand.

Roll paper napkins or doilies into a cone shape around the cake pops. This is a great way to package them for guests to take home after a party. Tie with ribbon if you like.

Stand cake pops upright in a cake, or round piece of styrofoam. Decorate the base to match the cake pops, using glitter, icing, wrapping paper or ribbon.

Fill mini pots, mugs, espresso cups or egg cups with lollies or marbles. Make sure you use something weighty so the cake pops stay upright.

Step-by-steps

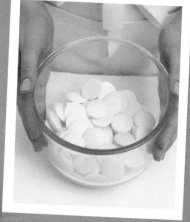

Melting chocolate on the stove Place chocolate in a glass bowl over a pan of simmering water; don't let water touch the base of bowl; stir occasionally.

Melting chocolate in the microwave Place chocolate in a microwave-safe bowl; heat on medium heat; stir often.

Melting chocolate Stir chocolate away from the heat until smooth. Microwaved chocolate will hold its shape, so check that it's melted by pressing with a spoon.

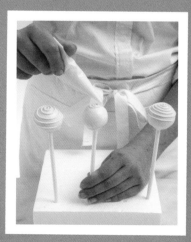

Creating pops Dip the end of a lollipop or paddle pop stick into the melted chocolate; push the stick about halfway into a ball of cake.

Coating pops Dip each cake pop into the melted chocolate; rock backwards and forwards to ensure they are evenly coated.

Baby rattles (p18) Pipe spirals of royal icing around the tops of the cake pops, turning them in the styrofoam as you pipe.

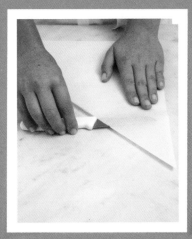

Piping bags Cut a square from baking paper, fold it in half diagonally. Cut paper along the fold to make two triangles.

Piping bags Hold apex of triangle towards you, wrap one point of triangle around to form a cone. Wrap remaining point around to make bag.

Piping bags Wriggle the points of the triangle together until they line up perfectly. Staple the bag to secure the three points in place.

Piping chocolate First make a paper piping bag (see above), then half-fill the bag with melted chocolate; fold over the top of the bag.

Piping chocolate Snip a tiny tip from the piping bag. Pipe chocolate, holding bag at a 45° angle. Pipe freehand or follow a pattern.

Pretty pink butterflies (p104) Using picture as a guide, pipe 50 x 6cm (2½-inch) single butterfly wings onto sheets of baking paper. Stand until set.

Wedding cakes (p48) Dip ends of the cake pop sticks into chocolate; push sticks through large rounds, extending about 4.5cm past the top of the cake.

Wedding cakes (p48) Dip all the tiers for the wedding cake into melted chocolate. Let excess chocolate drip off, then level under each tier with a knife.

Wedding cakes (p48) Push the medium and small tiers onto the extended cake pop stick; secure the tiers together with a little melted chocolate.

Top hats (p50) Push two of the cake rounds onto a chocolate-dipped cake pop stick to form the hats, joining rounds with a little melted chocolate.

Top hats (p50) Push a round of chocolate onto stick to make the brim of the hat. Secure brim to hat with a little melted chocolate.

Pistachio macaroon pops (p64) Gently transfer small pieces of silver leaf onto macaroons. Avoid touching the silver leaf as it will stick to your fingers.

Christmas ice-cream pops (p70) To make chocolate curls, warm the chocolate block between your hands; drag the blade of a sharp vegetable peeler down the side.

Toffee puff pops (p52) Quickly stir the ingredients together over heat, until the mixture forms a ball and pulls away from the side of the pan.

Toffee puff pops (p52) Transfer hot mixture to a medium heatproof bowl. Beat in the eggs, one at a time, adding the last egg as required.

Toffee puff pops (p52) Pipe or spoon the pastry onto greased or baking paper-lined trays. Leave about 5cm (2 inches) between each puff to allow for spreading.

Toffee puff pops (p52) After the puffs are cooked, immediately cut a small slit in the bottom to allow the steam to escape. Pipe filling through the slits in the puffs.

Toffee puff pops (p52) Working quickly, dip the puffs one at a time into the toffee. Use tongs or two forks to hold the puffs.

Glossary

ALMONDS

flaked paper-thin slices.

ground also called almond meal; nuts are powdered coarsely for use in baking or as a thickening agent.

BAKING PAPER also called parchment, silicon paper or non-stick baking paper; not to be confused with greaseproof paper. Used to line cake pans and make piping bags.

BAKING POWDER a raising agent consisting mainly of two parts cream of tartar to one part bicarbonate of (baking) soda.

BICARBONATE OF SODA also called baking soda; a mild alkali used as a leavening agent in baking.

BUTTER we use salted butter unless stated otherwise.

unsalted or "sweet" butter has no added salt.

CACHOUS also known as dragées; these minuscule (3mm to 5mm) metallic looking yet edible confectionery balls are available in silver, gold and some colours.

CANDY MELTS available from cake decorating suppliers; are easy-to-melt discs that are ideal for dipping and coating.

They come in a variety of colours and flavours and melt in the same way as chocolate.

CEREAL

Milo Duos malt- and vanilla-flavoured cereal curls, available in supermarkets.

CHOCOLATE

Choc Bits also called chocolate chips or chocolate morsels; available in milk, white and dark chocolate.

dark cooking also called compound chocolate; good for cooking as it doesn't require tempering and sets at room temperature.

dark eating also called semi-sweet or luxury chocolate; made of a high percentage of cocoa liquor and cocoa butter, with little added sugar.

milk eating most popular eating chocolate, mild and very sweet; similar in make-up to dark, with the difference being the addition of milk solids.

Melts small discs of compound milk, white or dark chocolate ideal for melting and moulding.

white eating contains no cocoa solids but derives its sweet flavour from cocoa butter. Very sensitive to heat.

CINNAMON available in pieces (sticks or quills) and ground into powder; one of the world's most common spices.

COCOA POWDER also called unsweetened cocoa; cocoa beans (cacao seeds) that have been fermented, roasted, shelled, ground into powder then cleared of most of the fat content.

COCONUT

desiccated dried, unsweetened, finely shredded coconut flesh.

flaked dried flakes of coconut flesh.

moist flakes sweetened, moistened coconut flakes.

shredded unsweetened thin strips of dried coconut flesh.

CORNFLOUR also known as cornstarch. Available made from corn or wheat (wheaten cornflour, gluten-free, gives a lighter texture in cakes); used as a thickening agent.

CREAM

pouring also called pure cream; has no additives.

thickened a whipping cream that contains a thickener.

EGGS we use large chicken eggs (60g) in our recipes unless stated otherwise. If a recipe calls for raw or barely cooked eggs, exercise caution if there is a salmonella problem in your area.

FLOUR

plain also called all-purpose; unbleached wheat flour is the best for baking.

self-raising all-purpose plain or wholemeal flour with baking powder and salt added.

strong baker's also known as gluten-enriched, baker's or bread-mix flour. Produced from a variety of wheat that has a high gluten (protein) content and is best suited for pizza and bread making. It is available from supermarkets and health food stores.

FOOD COLOURING vegetable-based substance available in liquid, paste or gel form.

ICE-CREAM use good-quality ice-cream where possible.

JAM also called conserve or preserve.

LOLLIES also called sweets or candy.

MILK we use full-cream homogenised milk unless stated otherwise.

POPCORN a variety of corn that is sold as kernels for popping, or can be bought ready-popped. Also available sweetened and coloured.

READY-MADE FROSTING also known as creamy deluxe frosting. Found in the baking section of most supermarkets; ready to spread straight from the tub. Available in flavours such as rich chocolate fudge, milk chocolate and vanilla.

READY-MADE WHITE ICING also known as ready-to-roll icing (RTR), fondant icing, sugar paste, plastic icing and soft icing. Is sweet tasting, and has a dough-like consistency when kneaded. Used to cover cakes and make decorations. Available from the baking section in most supermarkets.

ROSEWATER extract made from crushed rose petals; used for its aromatic quality in many desserts. Don't confuse with rose essence, which is more concentrated.

STYROFOAM a tightly-packed polystyrene foam that resists moisture. It is available in different-shaped blocks from cake decorating and craft supply stores.

SUGAR we use coarse, granulated table sugar, also called crystal sugar, unless stated otherwise.

brown a very soft, fine granulated sugar retaining molasses for its characteristic colour and flavour.

caster also known as superfine or finely granulated table sugar. The fine crystals dissolve easily making it perfect for cakes, meringues and desserts.

icing also called confectioners' sugar or powdered sugar; pulverised granulated sugar crushed together with a small amount of cornflour.

pure icing also called confectioners' or powdered sugar; does not contain any cornflour.

VANILLA

bean dried, long, thin pod from a tropical golden orchid; the minuscule black seeds inside the bean are used to impart a luscious vanilla flavour in baking and desserts.

essence obtained from vanilla beans infused in alcohol and water.

extract obtained from vanilla beans infused in water; a non-alcoholic version of essence.

VERMICELLI NOODLES dried rice noodles, usually used in asian cooking.

Conversion chart

measures

One Australian metric measuring cup holds approximately 250ml; one Australian metric tablespoon holds 20ml; one Australian metric teaspoon holds 5ml.

The difference between one country's measuring cups and another's is within a two- or three-teaspoon variance, and will not affect your cooking results. North America, New Zealand and the United Kingdom use a 15ml tablespoon.

All cup and spoon measurements are level. The most accurate way of measuring dry ingredients is to weigh them. When measuring liquids, use a clear glass or plastic jug with metric markings.

We use large eggs with an average weight of 60g.

dry measures

METRIC	IMPERIAL
15g	½oz
30g	1oz
60g	2oz
90g	3oz
125g	4oz (¼lb)
155g	5oz
185g	6oz
220g	7oz
250g	8oz (½lb)
280g	9oz
315g	10oz
345g	11oz
375g	12oz (¾lb)
410g	13oz
440g	14oz
470g	15oz
500g	16oz (1lb)
750g	24oz (1½lb)
1kg	32oz (2lb)

liquid measures

METRIC	IMPERIAL
30ml	1 fluid oz
60ml	2 fluid oz
100ml	3 fluid oz
125ml	4 fluid oz
150ml	5 fluid oz
190ml	6 fluid oz
250ml	8 fluid oz
300ml	10 fluid oz
500ml	16 fluid oz
600ml	20 fluid oz
1000ml (1 litre)	32 fluid oz

length measures

METRIC	IMPERIAL
3mm	⅛in
6mm	¼in
1cm	½in
2cm	¾in
2.5cm	1in
5cm	2in
6cm	2½in
8cm	3in
10cm	4in
13cm	5in
15cm	6in
18cm	7in
20cm	8in
23cm	9in
25cm	10in
28cm	11in
30cm	12in (1ft)

oven temperatures

The oven temperatures in this book are for conventional ovens; if you have a fan-forced oven, decrease the temperature by 10-20 degrees.

	°C (CELSIUS)	°F (FAHRENHEIT)
Very slow	120	250
Slow	150	300
Moderately slow	160	325
Moderate	180	350
Moderately hot	200	400
Hot	220	425
Very hot	240	475

The imperial measurements used in this book are approximate only. Metric/imperial conversions are approximate only. Measurements for cake pans are approximate only; using same-shaped cake pans of a similar size should not affect the outcome of your baking. We measure the inside top of the cake pan to determine sizes.